CUPCAKES

CUPCAKES

Truly delectable creations for every day, for special occasions
and for sharing with friends, with more than 75 ideas shown
step by step and 270 beautiful photographs

Carol Pastor

LORENZ BOOKS

Main front cover image shows raspberry buttercream – for recipe, see page 21.

This edition is published by Lorenz Books
an imprint of Anness Publishing Ltd
Hermes House
88–89 Blackfriars Road
London SE1 8HA
tel. 020 7401 2077; fax 020 7633 9499

www.lorenzbooks.com; www.annesspublishing.com

If you like the images in this book and would like to investigate using them for publishing, promotions or advertising, please visit our website www.practicalpictures.com for more information.

UK distributor: Book Trade Services; tel. 0116 2759086; fax 0116 2759090; uksales@booktradeservices.com; exportsales@booktradeservices.com
North American distributor: National Book Network; tel. 301 459 3366; fax 301 429 5746; www.nbnbooks.com
Australian distributor: Pan Macmillan Australia; tel. 1300 135 113; fax 1300 135 103; customer.service@macmillan.com.au
New Zealand distributor: David Bateman Ltd; tel. (09) 415 7664; fax (09) 415 8892

Publisher: Joanna Lorenz
Editorial Director: Helen Sudell
Editor: Simona Hill
Photographer: Craig Robertson
Stylist: Helen Trent
Designer: Simon Daley
Production Controller: Mai-Ling Collyer

ETHICAL TRADING POLICY

Because of our ongoing ecological investment programme, you, as our customer, can have the pleasure and reassurance of knowing that a tree is being cultivated on your behalf to naturally replace the materials used to make the book you are holding. For further information about this scheme, go to www.annesspublishing.com/trees

NOTES

- Bracketed terms are intended for American readers.
- For all recipes, quantities are given in both metric and imperial measures and, where appropriate, in standard cups and spoons. Follow one set, but not a mixture, because they are not interchangeable.
- Standard spoon and cup measures are level. 1 tsp = 5ml, 1 tbsp = 15ml, 1 cup = 250ml/8fl oz.
- Australian standard tablespoons are 20ml. Australian readers should use 3 tsp in place of 1 tbsp for measuring small quantities.
- The nutritional analysis given for each recipe is calculated per cake. If the recipe gives a range, such as Makes 8–9, then the nutritional analysis will be for the smaller size, i.e. 9 cakes. Optional ingredients and those added 'to taste' are not included.
- Large (US extra large) eggs are used unless otherwise stated.

ACKNOWLEDGEMENTS

The author and publishers would like to thank the following suppliers for the loan of equipment and provision of products which were used in the preparation of the recipes:

A la Cook – The Cook Shop
www.alacook.co.uk
De Longhi
www.delonghi.co.uk
Jane Asher Party Cakes & Sugarcraft
www.jane-asher.co.uk
Lakeland
www.lakeland.co.uk
Morphy Richards
www.morphyrichards.co.uk
Whitworths
www.whitworths-sugars.com

PUBLISHER'S NOTE

Contents

Introduction

Cupcakes were first made during the Victorian period, using a classic Victoria sponge recipe with simple decorations such as angelica, candied cherries and pineapple. These featherlight confections were named fairy cakes in Britain and were enjoyed with afternoon tea. American cooks made them larger, used rich buttercream flavoured with vanilla, blueberries or chocolate and named them cupcakes – possibly because the recipe for the sponge called for a cupful of each ingredient.

Today the names 'fairy cake' and 'cupcake' are almost interchangeable. They are a sweet cake that everyone recognizes and are guaranteed to evoke fond memories. These delightful cakes, each presented in individual portions, appeal to our sense of nostalgia. They represent comfort food, a sweet treat, and are often associated with memories of childhood attempts at home baking. Today these confections have caught the public imagination. Timeless recipes for vanilla, lemon, chocolate and cherry cakes have become the mainstay of tearooms and cafés everywhere, from country tea gardens to über-trendy city patisseries. They are the perfect recipe to serve for afternoon tea, to dress up with fruit and ice cream as a divine dessert, and to fill with mouthfuls of indulgent creamy icing. They have become, too, the centrepiece for christenings and anniversaries.

Below For the ultimate cupcake, arrange moulded sugarpaste flowers and cut-out butterflies on top of a cake and present it in a fine bone china teacup.

Above Zigzag lines of piped chocolate make an attractive topping for chocolate or coffee-flavoured cupcakes. Pipe the lines directly on the cake or over an iced topping.

For cakes that are to stand on a cake tower, for wedding breakfasts or anniversary parties, pale, understated colours such as ivory, pale peach, shell pink or white often look most pleasing. A pale green pistachio cupcake dusted with icing sugar through a simple leaf stencil has breathtaking appeal; deep purple violets fresh from the garden look exquisite with a cream cheese topping, or you could finish a simple chocolate cake with a dark truffle rolled in cocoa powder. For those with a more creative spirit, a pattern of spring flowers embossed on almond paste would make a lovely decoration for a batch of spicy Easter cakes.

Look out for antique wooden butter moulds, biscuit (cookie) moulds or small wooden fabric printing blocks. They make unique templates to impress patterns in soft marzipan or sugarpaste toppings – a simple and effective decoration.

Don't forget that delicious and inventive ingredients will turn an everyday cupcake into something special, and be ready to try imaginative variations on a simple theme. Instead of grated orange rind, try whole boiled clementines, puréed to add an intense tangy flavour. You could replace ground almonds with ground chestnuts, or add exotic fruits, as well as wonderful quince paste to enhance apple and pear cakes. Sometimes liqueurs add a rounded flavour, and you could replace brandy with grappa, or lemon with limoncello. But don't get too serious. Cupcakes should be fun as well as visually pleasing. Coloured candy sugar makes a cake crumb pink within, and pretty yellow sugarpaste daisies, moulded marzipan fruits and brightly coloured marbled sugarpaste seashells all make irresistible toppings. For children's parties little alphabet sweets are always a great success. The children will take delight in helping you press their initials into the luscious icing.

To enjoy them at their best, small cakes should be eaten on the day or the day after they are made. Most can be successfully frozen, if necessary, but not citrus syrup cakes or those with meringue or fresh fruit. Defrosted cakes improve if you lightly warm them through just before serving to regain their fresh-out-of-the oven texture: a minute or less on low power in the microwave is all they need.

Some of the recipes in the book call for cupcakes or fairy cakes to be made in a muffin tin (pan): this gives taller, more straight-sided cakes than a bun tin, which

Above **Plain cupcakes can be made to look original, with a** *fine dusting of icing sugar sprinkled over a paper doily to create a lacy effect on top of the cake.*

has shallower cups with sloping sides. Some bun tins have larger cups than others – buy larger ones if you have a choice. You will need to line the tins with paper cases: a little smear of butter in the base of each cup will secure the cases and make it easier to fill them.

The presentation of the cakes finishes the picture. You can wrap them in beautiful card cake cups, decorated with pastel coloured paper doves, or pack them in a box tied with thin coloured ribbons, ready to give to a friend or loved one. You can even make your own pretty labels to personalize your creations.

Whether you choose muffin-style cupcakes (maybe with a spoonful of sweetened crème fraîche and a piece of fresh fruit), moist gluten-free citrus syrup cupcakes, sweet and sticky enough to eat with cream as a pudding, or the classic fairy cake, each is sure to offer a tiny morsel of sweet pleasure. So if you are deciding what to bake for your next tea party, beach party, children's birthday, wedding breakfast or friends' reunion, or even if you just want something delicious to eat with a pot of tea at your own kitchen table with a friend, this book has plenty of simple, creative and elegant ideas.

Left **Mounds of fresh fruit piled on top of a small cupcake** *make a decadent dessert. Serve with fresh cream, ice cream or both.*

Ingredients

Always use the best ingredients you can afford to buy, as their quality will give your cakes a really special aroma and fine flavour. Here is a guide to the ingredients that are essential for making delicious cupcakes and fairy cakes.

Baking powder This mixture of two parts acidic cream of tartar and one part alkaline bicarbonate of soda is a raising agent. When mixed with a liquid and heated, it releases carbon dioxide, which makes cakes rise. Store it in a sealed container in a dry place because any moisture will activate it. It must be mixed evenly into flour when baking: do this by sifting it twice with the flour.

Butter There is no substitute for the rich creamy taste of fresh butter. For creaming, it should be at room temperature. It is soft enough for beating when your forefinger pressed into the butter leaves a soft impression. In cold weather soften it in the microwave on low power for about 15 seconds. If you use salted butter you may not need to add the "pinch of salt" referred to in the ingredients list in some recipes.

Buttermilk Traditional buttermilk is the whey produced when butter is churned from cream, but nowadays it is generally made by adding acidic cultures to skimmed milk. It has a tangy off-sweet flavour, which is good in scones or muffins. Apart from balancing an over-sweet cake mixture, the acid it contains helps trigger the carbon dioxide reaction to ensure well-risen cakes.

Cream Fresh whipped double (heavy) cream needs sweetening to balance the sweetness of the cake, and can be flavoured with vanilla, caramel, coffee, chocolate, lemon curd or fruit liqueurs. Avoid over-whipping double cream, as it can separate when it is piped.

Crème fraîche This cream has a delicate sourness that works as a topping on sweeter cakes. It can be flavoured in the same way as cream.

Eggs Whole beaten eggs are used for thickening cake mixtures and lightening the texture. For flavour, free range or organic eggs are the preferred choice. Large (US extra large) eggs are used in these recipes.

Dried fruit Don't store dried fruit for too long; the fruits should be succulent and tender.

Flour Self-raising (self-rising) flour produces a fine grain when baked. To make your own, add 5ml/1 tsp baking powder to every 115g/4oz plain (all-purpose) flour. Self-raising flour may lose some of its raising potential if it is stored for too long: use within 4 months of purchase for best results. Plain flour is also used in cake making but it is usually necessary to add a raising agent.

Food colouring Use liquid colouring for glacé icing unless a very rich colour is required, when you should use a paste. Always use paste for colouring sugarpaste to preserve its firm consistency. Add just a few drops or specks.

Below The basic ingredients: flour, eggs, butter and sugar.

Below Icing (confectioners') sugar, fondant icing and marzipan.

Below Cake flavourings include coffee, cocoa and natural extracts.

Fresh fruit Tart-sweet berries, fresh figs, apples and cherries add a juiciness and natural flavour to cakes. The juice of strawberries or raspberries will colour icing pink and add a lovely fruity flavour. The grated rind and juice of a lemon or orange gives a fantastic citrus lift and can balance an over-sweet cake.

Jam To make a glaze, simmer together 45ml/3 tbsp sieved apricot jam, 15–30ml/1–2 tbsp water and 30ml/2 tbsp sugar until thickened. This can be brushed over cakes or fruit toppings to add gloss and extra flavour, or used to glue marzipan to the cake tops. Quince jam glaze, made in the same way, is suitable for cakes baked with quince slices, apples or pears; redcurrant jelly glaze will enhance red berries.

Nuts Whichever you choose, nuts add a distinctive flavour and texture to cake mixtures. Ground almonds are indispensable for adding a rich moistness to cakes.

Rose or orange flower water The heady scents of roses, scented geranium and orange blossom are distilled into bottles for cooking. One teaspoon of a pure extract is

sufficient to add a noticeable fragrance to a dozen small cakes.

Royal icing This type of icing sets hard, and is good for attaching sugarpaste decorations. Sift 250g/9oz/ 2¹⁄₄ cups icing (confectioners') sugar into a bowl and make a well in the centre. Add 1 egg white, lightly beaten, and 15ml/1 tbsp lemon juice; whisk until stiff and glossy.

Spices Whole spices, freshly ground, deliver the finest flavour and will last longer if they are stored in a sealed container away from light. Spices bought ready ground will last for up to 6 months.

Spirits and liqueurs are used in some recipes. Crème de framboise (raspberry liqueur) goes well with cakes containing red berries; Calvados (apple brandy) is ideal for fruit cakes made with quince, pear or apples. Limoncello (lemon liqueur) suits most citrus-based cakes and grappa (an Italian aperitif made with grapes) has a special affinity with marzipan and almonds.

Sugar Caster (superfine) sugar is indispensable in cake making because its very fine crystals dissolve

easily. The pale grains of organic or golden caster sugar add a light caramelized flavour. Granulated sugar has larger crystals and is ideal for cooking fruits, boiled syrups and caramel. Light soft brown sugar has a mild molasses flavour and gives a deep golden crumb. Brown sugar has no nutritional advantage over white unless specified as 'unrefined', but some people prefer the taste. Candy sugar, or caster sugar tinted with food colouring, makes a pretty decoration sprinkled over cakes.

Sugarpaste (rolled fondant) is easily sculpted or rolled and shaped with cutters. You can make your own, but ready-made sugarpaste is of excellent quality. Keep it well wrapped as it dries very quickly. Coloured sugarpastes are available, and are useful if you require a very strong colour. Otherwise, it is more practical to tint the paste with a few drops of food colouring.

Vanilla Occasionally you may find pure vanilla bean paste (vanilla extract and beans crushed into a syrupy paste). More readily available is real vanilla extract, with a more distinct flowery aroma than essence, which is synthetic and cheaper.

Below Sprinkles are fun to use and available in lots of designs.

Below Always buy a quality brand of chocolate for best results.

Below Paste and liquid colours can both be used for cupcakes.

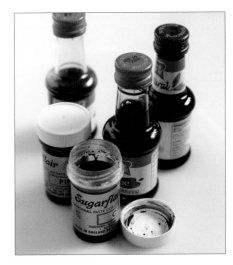

Equipment

Bakers are only as good as their tools, so use good quality utensils whenever possible. They are more satisfying to use and more efficient. An interesting selection of small decorative moulds and cutters will add an extra creative dimension to your cakes and make them visually memorable.

Canelle knife This is a type of zester that cuts fine spaghetti-like strands from hard-skinned citrus fruits. Use the strands to decorate the tops of lemon- or orange-flavoured cakes.

Decorative cutters A graded set of plain and scalloped cutters is used in some of the recipes. Dip them into icing sugar to prevent the sugarpaste or marzipan sticking to them when you stamp out circles for the tops of cupcakes. Choose good quality steel cutters for accurate circles – blunt ones will compress the edges. Shaped cutters – leaves, flowers, rabbits, Christmas trees, letters and numerals – are useful. Plunger cutters are particularly good for producing really professional-looking flowers and leaf shapes with detailed veins. They are available from specialist sugarcraft shops and some good cookware suppliers.

Below You will need a range of mixing bowls – small, medium and large – for sifting ingredients, creaming mixtures, whipping cream and making icing.

Dredger This is a metal container with a fine gauze lid in which you can store icing sugar. Use it to dust the work surface when working with marzipan and rolled sugarpaste. Because it has a finer gauze than a kitchen sieve it is better for adding a fine last-minute dusting of icing sugar or cocoa powder.

Food mixer This is great for beating together butter, sugar and eggs, but it is advisable to fold in the dry ingredients by hand. Buy an extra mixing bowl if you can, to avoid having to wash the bowl halfway through. Some mixers have a liquidizer attachment, which is useful for fruit purées.

Hand-held electric whisk Useful for making quick buttercream and whipped cream, it can also be used in a pan over heat for meringue-based recipes.

Below Invest in heavy-gauge, good quality muffin and bun tins (pans) for perfect results, and always cool cakes on wire racks.

Measuring spoons Exact spoon measurements are vital, particularly for baking powder, vanilla extract, spices, orange and rose waters.

Mixing bowls Choose bowls that fit inside one another. Many are attractive enough to sit out on the kitchen surface, close to hand, rather than be packed away in a cupboard.

Moulds These are used to form small pieces of coloured marzipan into intricate cake decorations. Look for small antique chocolate moulds, decorative wooden fabric printing stamps, or wooden butter moulds for embossing cupcake toppings.

Muffin and bun tins (pans) can be made of metal or silicone rubber. Silicone has a controlled flexibility that makes it easy to release the cakes. Muffin cups are usually taller and straighter than bun cups, which have sloping sides.

Below A piping bag and nozzles are essential cake decorating tools.

Palette knife or metal spatula For spreading and smoothing icing and creating swirls or peaks in cream and buttercream.

Paper Non-stick siliconized baking parchment is useful for inter-leaving cakes and decorations in storage boxes. Silicone paper can also be used to make flat iced shapes to be applied to the top of cakes after they are dry.

Paper cake cases Finely pleated cake papers are convenient for easy release from the tins (pans) and help to keep the cakes fresher. Make sure they are non-stick or most of the cake will stick to the paper. Use the cases double for neater cakes, and treble if free-standing on a baking sheet.

Pastry brush Look out for wide, soft brushes that will cover the whole surface of a cupcake in one sweep when adding a hot jam glaze or brushing over royal icing as a fixing agent for toppings. You will also need a smaller artist's brush for sticking on cake decorations.

Piping (pastry) bags These are made of fabric or polyester and are fitted with piping nozzles. Small

Below Use plunger cutters and modelling tools for intricate decorations.

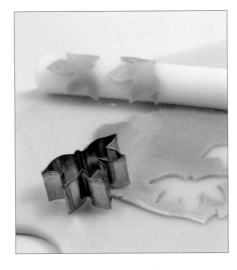

Above A smooth, small rolling pin and work board make handling tiny shapes easy.

baking parchment piping bags are used for piping thin lines or small decorations – just snip off the tip of the bag rather than using a nozzle.

Sieve (strainer) (wire or plastic) Essential for sifting flour and raising agents together, and for sifting icing (confectioners') sugar when making smooth icing or buttercream. Have at least two – one for dry ingredients and another for wet ones.

Stencils and templates You can buy these ready-made, but you can also cut out your own shapes, such as

Below Good quality sharp steel cutters are available in dozens of shapes.

Above To make light and airy sponge cakes and for speed, an electric mixer is a good kitchen standby.

birds, stars and flowers, from heavy duty tracing paper or thin cardboard.

Weighing scales Invest in a good set of scales able to weigh small or large quantities with precision.

Wire racks are essential to allow the steam to escape easily from the hot cakes. A circular wire rack can also be used as a stencil to make a spider's web pattern if placed over the top of a cake and sprinkled with a dusting of icing sugar. Use the rack of a grill (broiler) pan as a surface on which to cool cakes, if you like.

Below Paper and foil cases are made in a range of sizes, colours and patterns.

Basic recipes

Cupcakes are simple to make and decorate. This chapter shows you how to create perfect portions of sweet cake with which to tantalize your tastebuds and impress your friends. Two simple methods for making basic cakes are included, and there are recipes for colourful and indulgent buttercream, sugarpaste and marzipan toppings, as well as easy decorations that add a sense of fun to baking.

Basic cupcake recipe: creamed method

In this cake-making method the butter is beaten with the sugar until very creamy, then combined with the flour and flavourings. The resulting cake has a moist, dense crumb. The beating can be done with a wooden spoon or an electric mixer – the latter is less time-consuming.

MAKES 8–9

175g/6oz/³/₄ cup butter, softened
175g/6oz/³/₄ cup caster
  (superfine) sugar
5ml/1 tsp vanilla extract, or 5ml/
  1 tsp finely grated lemon rind
4 eggs, lightly beaten
175g/6oz/1¹/₂ cups self-raising (self-
  rising) flour, sifted

1 Preheat the oven to 180°C/350°F/ Gas 4. Line 8–9 cups of a bun tin (pan) with paper cases. Place the butter and sugar in a mixing bowl.

2 Beat together with a wooden spoon or an electric mixer until very light and creamy. Add the vanilla or lemon rind. Gradually add the eggs, beating well after each addition.

3 Add the sifted flour and fold it delicately into the mixture with a large spoon until just combined.

4 Divide the mixture among the paper cases and bake for 20 minutes until the cakes are golden brown and the centres feel firm to the touch. Remove from the oven.

5 Leave to cool for 5 minutes, then turn the cakes out on to a wire rack to cool completely before icing and decorating them.

6 These cupcakes are decorated by making a quantity of glacé icing and tinting it palest pink. Keep the consistency of the icing thick and pour on top of the cakes as soon as it is made. Decorate the surface with your choice of jellies.

Energy 317kcal/1326kJ; Protein 4.7g; Carbohydrate 35g, of which sugars 20.6g; Fat 18.6g, of which saturates 11.2g; Cholesterol 129mg; Calcium 94mg; Fibre 0.6g; Sodium 248mg.

Basic cupcake recipe: melting method

Here the butter is melted and left to cool slightly. The remaining cake ingredients are combined, and the cooled, melted butter is beaten in last. The resulting cakes will have a soft sponge-like texture and will rise evenly to give a flat top suitable for glacé icing and sugarpaste toppings.

MAKES 10

2 eggs
115g/4oz/¹/₂ cup caster (superfine)
  sugar
50ml/2fl oz/¹/₄ cup double (heavy)
  cream
finely grated rind of 1 lemon
115g/4oz/1 cup self-raising (self-
  rising) flour
2.5ml/¹/₂ tsp baking powder
50g/2oz/4 tbsp butter, melted

1 Preheat the oven to 180°C/350°F/ Gas 4 and line 10 holes of a bun tin (pan) with paper cases. Beat the eggs with the sugar. Beat in the cream for 1 minute, then add the lemon rind.

2 Sift the flour with the baking powder, then fold it lightly into the mixture, followed by the butter.

3 Three-quarters fill the paper cases with the cake mixture. Bake in the centre of the oven for 12–15 minutes until risen and golden brown. Test by lightly pressing the centres of the cakes with your fingers: the sponge should lightly spring back.

4 Remove from the oven and leave to cool in the bun tin for 5 minutes, then turn the cakes out on to a wire rack to cool completely before icing and decorating them.

5 These cupcakes are decorated with glacé icing. Either spread a thin layer on top and add piped lines or pipe straight on to the cakes.

Energy 157kcal/660kJ; Protein 2.4g; Carbohydrate 20.9g, of which sugars 12.3g; Fat 8g, of which saturates 4.5g; Cholesterol 56mg; Calcium 55mg; Fibre 0.4g; Sodium 95mg.

Glacé icing

Also known as water icing, this is the simplest of all icing recipes, and is ideal for decorating small cakes. It's quick to mix, with only two basic ingredients, and provided you take care to get the consistency right it flows easily over the surface and sets to a glossy smoothness.

Glacé icing, made with finely sifted icing (confectioners') sugar and hot water, makes a basic topping that is suitable for many cakes. The icing can be flavoured with vanilla, fruit juice and zest, chocolate, coffee or alcohol, and looks wonderful in delicate, pastel colours. It is important to get the consistency exactly right: too thick and it will not form a super-smooth glossy coating; too thin and it will run over the top and down the sides of the cake. Glacé icing sets to form a crisp surface, but never becomes rock hard. The consistency determines how many cakes the icing covers.

MAKES ENOUGH FOR 16 CUPCAKES

225g/8oz/2 cups icing (confectioners') sugar
15–30ml/1–2 tbsp hot water
a few drops of food colouring

Below Icing can be tinted with liquid or paste colours.

1 Sift the icing sugar into a bowl, then gradually mix in the water, a few drops at a time, beating until the mixture is the consistency of cream.

2 Add one or two drops of food colouring (with caution). For a more vibrant colour use paste food colouring, available from specialist suppliers. Stir until evenly coloured.

3 Use the icing immediately, while it is smooth and fluid. Add any further decoration before the icing dries.

VARIATIONS
Fresh fruit flavouring The strained juice from fresh berries such as raspberries, redcurrants or citrus fruits can be used to scent and softly colour plain icing and glazes. A more concentrated citrus hit can be achieved by adding finely grated rind or replacing some of the water used to make up the glacé icing with fruit juice.

Melting liqueur fondant Lift the flavour of icing with 15–30ml/1–2 tbsp crème de framboise (raspberry liqueur), limoncello (lemon liqueur), or another fruit-based liqueur, which will add fruity tones.

Iced fruit Small bunches of redcurrants or cherries (with their stalks left on) dipped in melting liqueur fondant and left to set on baking parchment make a very appealing and seasonal topping for summer cakes.

Opposite top left Alphabet decorations and tinted glacé icing make these cupcakes appealing to children.

Opposite top right Modelled sugar roses add the finishing touch to these Mother's Day cupcakes.

Opposite bottom left Real daisy petals add a delicate charm to these cakes.

Opposite bottom right Sprinkles are available in many shapes and colours.

Crystallized flower decorations

This traditional method of preserving summer flowers is simple to do and makes charming and very effective decorations for delicately iced cupcakes. The results can be spectacular, with prettily faded colours and the lingering perfumes of summer.

Popular edible flowers include primroses, violets, cowslips, alpine pinks and roses. Try bright blue anchusa, starry-petalled borage or vivid-red pineapple sage.

Use them individually or try different combinations. Some flowers, such as primroses, cowslips, borage, sage and anchusa, are easy to pull away from their green calyx and can be crystallized whole. Daisies, roses and pinks are often best divided into individual petals, although you might consider treating entire small flowerheads for a real showpiece. Fresh crystallized flowers that retain their moisture need using quickly, but flowers that are dried thoroughly in a warm place for 24–36 hours prior to crystallizing will last for a few months.

selection of petals and/or flowers
1 egg white
50g/2oz/¼ cup caster (superfine) sugar

1 Gather flowers when they are dry, and select clean, perfect specimens. Trim and prepare individual petals or whole flowers. Beat the egg white lightly and put it and the sugar in separate saucers.

2 Pick up each petal or flower and paint the entire surface, front and back, carefully with the egg white, using an artist's brush.

3 Dredge on both sides with caster sugar so that it sticks to the egg white and coats the flower or petal.

4 Lay the flowers and petals on baking parchment and leave them in a warm, dry place until completely dry and crisp. Store in a sealed container.

WARNING
Raw eggs should not be eaten by pregnant women, babies, young children or the elderly. If in doubt, use powdered egg white for coating the flowers. It will work just as well.

Vanilla buttercream

Buttercream is a clear favourite for filling and decorating sponge cakes as its rich sweet taste complements the plainest of cakes, and the basic recipe can be flavoured with almost anything you choose. This is a vanilla version, and others are given on the following pages.

FILLS 8–9 CUPCAKES

75g/3oz/6 tbsp butter, softened
175g/6oz/1½ cups icing
    (confectioners') sugar, double
    sifted, plus extra for dusting
½ vanilla pod (bean), split, or a
    few drops of vanilla extract
food colouring (optional)

1 To make buttercream, use butter that has had time to reach room temperature. Beat it well before beating in the sifted icing sugar. Ensure that no lumps remain.

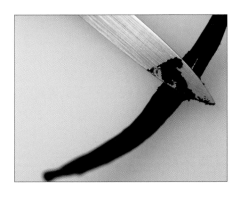

2 For the best vanilla flavour, split a vanilla pod in half and scrape out the seeds. Discard the pod and mix the seeds into the buttercream. Alternatively, add a few drops of vanilla extract to the mixture. Colour the icing, if you like, with a little colouring.

3 When the cakes have cooled, carefully cut round the lightly domed tops with a small sharp knife and remove the top of each cake. Slice the tops in half to form two semicircles, to make the butterfly wings. Set aside.

4 Use a piping (icing) bag with a star nozzle to pipe a whirl into each cake. Press the wings into the cream and dust with sifted icing sugar.

Energy 455kcal/1905kJ; Protein 4.8g; Carbohydrate 55.3g, of which sugars 40.9g; Fat 25.4g, of which saturates 15.7g; Cholesterol 148mg; Calcium 106mg; Fibre 0.6g; Sodium 312mg.

Luxurious vanilla cream

This is a light, ultra-smooth topping for a special occasion.

MAKES ENOUGH TO COVER 8 CUPCAKES

175g/6oz/¾ cup caster (superfine) sugar
3 egg whites
175g/6oz/¾ cup butter, softened
½ vanilla pod (bean), split

1 Put 45ml/3 tbsp water into a pan with the sugar and heat gently until dissolved. Bring to the boil and boil until it reaches 121°C/250°F. Remove from the heat.

2 Beat the egg whites until the mixture holds its shape in peaks. Gradually pour the syrup in a thin steady stream over the egg whites, whisking constantly at a low speed. until the meringue is thick and cold (about 10–15 minutes), then set aside.

3 In a separate bowl, beat the butter until it is creamy. Gradually add the meringue a large spoonful at a time with the vanilla seeds, whisking well after each addition.

Chestnut and dark chocolate cream

Chestnuts add an extra dimension to this rich icing.

MAKES ENOUGH TO COVER 12 CUPCAKES

175g/6oz/¾ cup butter, softened
115g/4oz/1 cup icing (confectioners') sugar, sifted
175g/6oz can puréed chestnuts
115g/4oz dark (bittersweet) chocolate, melted

1 In a large bowl, whisk the butter until soft and creamy. Whisking at a low speed, gradually add the icing sugar and the chestnut purée in alternate spoonfuls.

2 Continue to beat the mixture, adding the cooled melted chocolate, until the icing is thick and creamy.

VARIATION
Substitute 115g/4oz/½ cup of mascarpone for the dark chocolate if you want a lighter buttercream.

Left: Energy 252kcal/1049kJ; Protein 1.3g; Carbohydrate 22.9g, of which sugars 22.9g; Fat 17.8g, of which saturates 11.8g; Cholesterol 50mg; Calcium 16mg; Fibre 0g; Sodium 188mg.
Right: Energy 220kcal/918kJ; Protein 0.8g; Carbohydrate 21.6g, of which sugars 16.7g; Fat 15.1g, of which saturates 9.6g; Cholesterol 34mg; Calcium 17mg; Fibre 0.6g; Sodium 113mg.

Raspberry buttercream

This mouthwatering raspberry pink cream is great for party cakes, when it is piped into little rosettes.

MAKES ENOUGH TO COVER 12 CUPCAKES

175g/6oz/¾ cup butter, softened
350g/12oz/3 cups icing (confectioners') sugar, sifted
25ml/1½ tbsp lemon juice
25ml/1½ tbsp raspberry jam
few drops red food colouring (optional)

1 In a bowl, beat the butter with the icing sugar until smooth and fluffy.

2 Stir in the lemon juice and raspberry jam and continue to beat until smooth. (Sieve the jam if you prefer to exclude the seeds from the mixture.)

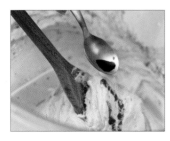

3 Add a few drops of food colouring if you wish and beat until the buttercream is evenly coloured a soft raspberry pink.

Lemon crème fraîche buttercream

This is a fresh, zesty topping, suitable for lemon-based cakes. Decorate with candied lemon rind, and dust with icing sugar.

MAKES ENOUGH TO COVER 12 CUPCAKES

140g/5oz/10 tbsp butter, softened
350g/12oz/3 cups icing (confectioners') sugar, sifted
140g/5oz/⅔ cup crème fraîche
juice of 1 lemon
finely grated rind of 2 lemons

1 Put the softened butter in a mixing bowl. Whisking at a low speed, gradually add the icing sugar and crème fraîche in alternate amounts.

2 Continue to beat the mixture with a wooden spoon, adding the lemon juice and grated lemon rind, until thick and creamy, about 3 minutes.

3 Cover the bowl and chill the buttercream for at least 1 hour before using, to firm up slightly.

Left: Energy 228kcal/955kJ; Protein 0.2g; Carbohydrate 31.9g, of which sugars 1.9g; Fat 11.9g, of which saturates 7.8g; Cholesterol 34mg; Calcium 18mg; Fibre 0g; Sodium 111mg.
Right: Energy 245kcal/1025kJ; Protein 0.5g; Carbohydrate 307.6g, of which sugars 30.7g; Fat 14.2g, of which saturates 9.5g; Cholesterol 40mg; Calcium 24mg; Fibre 0g; Sodium 92mg.

Seville orange buttercream

A few drops of Grand Marnier will add warmth to the flavour of this sharp-sweet butter frosting. Out of season, a sweet orange may be substituted for the Seville orange.

MAKES ENOUGH TO COVER 8 CUPCAKES

140g/5oz/10 tbsp butter, softened
250g/9oz/2¼ cups icing (confectioners') sugar
juice and finely grated rind of one Seville orange
5ml/1 tsp Grand Marnier
orange food colouring (optional)

1 Beat the softened butter until light and fluffy, using an electric mixer or a wooden spoon.

2 Gradually add the sugar, orange juice and rind, Grand Marnier and a few drops of food colouring, if using, beating continuously until the mixture is smooth.

3 Cover the bowl and chill for several hours to allow the flavours to mature before using as a filling or topping.

Pistachio and rose water buttercream

Rose water and pistachios have a subtle affinity.

MAKES ENOUGH TO COVER 8 CUPCAKES

115g/4oz/¾ cup pistachio nuts, shelled
140g/5oz/10 tbsp butter
115g/4oz/1 cup icing (confectioners') sugar, sifted
10ml/2 tsp milk
2–3 drops rose water, or to taste

1 Process the pistachio nuts in a blender or food processor until very finely ground.

2 Whisk the butter until soft and creamy. Whisking at a low speed, gradually beat in the sugar, pistachios and milk, alternating with the rose water, until smooth.

COOK'S TIP
Remove pistachio skins by blanching the nuts for a few seconds in boiling water, then rubbing them in a clean dish towel while still warm.

Left: Energy 255kcal/1070kJ; Protein 0.3g; Carbohydrate 33.2g, of which sugars 33.2g; Fat 14.3g, of which saturates 9.5g; Cholesterol 40mg; Calcium 20mg; Fibre 0.1g; Sodium 134mg.
Right: Energy 356kcal/1475kJ; Protein 5.3g; Carbohydrate 17.5g, of which sugars 17g; Fat 30g, of which saturates 11.6g; Cholesterol 40mg; Calcium 44mg; Fibre 1.7g; Sodium 282mg.

American cream cheese frosting

Don't confine this famous cream cheese buttercream to spicy carrot cake. It also makes a splendid topping for fudgy chocolate or ginger cakes, and is so delicious you might end up eating it all before it ever gets to top your cupcakes.

MAKES ENOUGH TO COVER 12 CUPCAKES

140g/5oz/10 tbsp butter, softened
225g/8oz/1 cup cream cheese
225–250g/8–9oz/2–2¼ cups icing (confectioners')
  sugar, sifted
5ml/1 tsp finely grated lemon rind (optional)

1 Beat the butter and cream cheese together until thoroughly blended, soft and creamy.

2 Gradually beat in the icing sugar until the mixture is smooth, with a spreadable consistency that holds a soft peak. Mix in the grated lemon rind, if using.

Espresso coffee and mascarpone buttercream

This soft Italian cream cheese topping, with a pronounced coffee flavour, is suitable for coffee or nut-based cakes. Enjoy!

MAKES ENOUGH TO COVER 12 CUPCAKES

175g/6oz/¾ cup butter, softened
2.5ml/½ tsp finely grated lemon rind
350g/12oz/3 cups icing (confectioners') sugar, sifted
225g/8oz/1 cup mascarpone
10ml/2 tsp double-strength espresso coffee

1 Beat the butter in a bowl until soft. Add the lemon rind and gradually mix in the sugar and mascarpone alternately, in small amounts, smooth and creamy. Stir in the coffee.

COOK'S TIP
Powdered strong instant coffee dissolved in 15ml/1 tbsp boiling water can be substituted for the espresso, if you like.

Left: Energy 240kcal/1000kJ; Protein 0.7g; Carbohydrate 28.7g, of which sugars 19.2g; Fat 18.4g, of which saturates 11.9g; Cholesterol 45mg; Calcium 30mg; Fibre 0g; Sodium 145mg.
Right: Energy 256kcal/1072kJ; Protein 2g; Carbohydrate 31g, of which sugars 31.1g; Fat 14.6g, of which saturates 9.5g; Cholesterol 41mg; Calcium 17mg; Fibre 0g; Sodium 111mg.

Working with sugarpaste

A versatile medium for all kinds of edible ornaments, sugarpaste can be rolled out like pastry and used to cover cakes of all sizes with a perfect, smooth sweet coating. It can also be stamped, embossed and moulded to make a wonderful range of three-dimensional decorations.

Sugarpaste, also known as fondant, is a combination of liquid glucose, gelatine, glycerine and icing (confectioners') sugar, and can be bought ready-made. You can make it at home, but the availability of some excellent products on the market means it is more convenient to buy it. Sugarpaste is sold vacuum packed in plastic bags. When you use it make sure that during and after use you keep it well wrapped with plastic wrap, or it will become dry and chalky in texture and unusable. If the paste is too sticky, add a little finely sifted icing sugar to it.

To tint sugarpaste

Subtle tones of sugarpaste often look much more appealing than bright ones, especially if the cakes are for an elegant celebration. If you require a vibrant colour it is better to buy it ready coloured from a sugarcraft shop, because the quantities of colour needed make the paste too wet.

1 To colour sugarpaste add a few drops of food colour or a few specks of paste to a ball of sugarpaste. Knead until the colour is evenly distributed.

To mould sugarpaste shapes

Plastic chocolate moulds are a good investment for this skill. The fine texture of sugarpaste makes it ideal for shaping intricate decorative moulds.

1 Place the paste on a working surface lightly dusted with sifted icing sugar, and knead until it is smooth and free from cracks. Colour it as required.

2 Divide the paste into portions and press each into a decorative mould. Press repeatedly to ensure the paste adheres. Trim the top so that it is smooth and level.

3 Chill for several hours. Press the tip of a knife between the paste and the mould to create an air pocket. Prise out the shape and leave to defrost. Smooth out any knife marks once the sugarpaste has softened sufficiently.

To make sugarpaste plunger-cut flowers

With a flower cutter, such as a plunger cutter, you can make perfect small flowers quickly. The plunge mechanism in each cutter pushes the flower out of the cutter and makes the shape of each cupped. You just need to add a contrasting centre to finish them off.

1 Lightly dust the work surface with sifted icing sugar. Roll out a small ball of coloured sugarpaste to ¹/₈in/3mm thick using a small rolling pin.

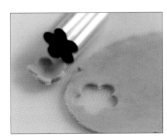

2 Use a plunger cutter (available in different flower shapes) to cut out flowers and lift them gently from the surface using a flat palette knife or metal spatula to avoid squashing the edges of the petals with your fingers.

3 Using a fine plain nozzle and a small quantity of royal icing in a piping bag, pipe a small blob at the centre of each flower.

To make stamped sugarpaste flowers

Shaped small-scale cutters are available to suit every theme.

1 Roll out a small ball of coloured fondant on a light dusting of icing sugar to 3mm/¹/₈in thick and cut out each shape.

2 Use a ball modelling tool to gently manipulate the sugarpaste flowers into a cup shape, bending the petals up a little. Pipe the centre and add false stamens if you like.

To emboss sugarpaste

Imprint patterns in soft sugarpaste with decorative tools.

1 Use a decorative rolling pin or craft stamp, available from sugarcraft shops, and press firmly on to thinly rolled out paste to leave an imprint. Remove with care.

2 Use a cookie cutter to cut a scalloped circle. Stick to the top of a cupcake with a little royal icing.

Working with marzipan

Redolent of medieval feasts, marzipan is a luxurious confection made from ground almonds and fine sugar and is used for covering cakes and making sweets, often coloured and shaped into little fruits, flowers and animals. It can be flavoured with rose or orange flower water.

Marzipan leaves

Marzipan is an ideal material for cutting and moulding decorative shapes such as small pumpkins and other vegetables, fruit, flowers or leaves, all of which make exquisite small decorations for cupcakes. Small leaves made from rolled-out marzipan can make stunning cake decorations, used by themselves or combined with crystallized or sugarpaste flowers. Try green holly leaves on Christmas cupcakes, or these autumnal oak leaves.

MAKES 8–10 LEAVES

50g/2oz marzipan, tinted as desired
icing (confectioners') sugar, for dusting

1 Roll out the marzipan thinly. Cut out leaves with a cutter, or cut round a card template using a craft knife. Leave to dry on baking parchment.

2 For curled leaves, drape the shapes over a rolling pin and leave to dry at room temperature for 2 days. Paint the veins and edges with food colouring using a fine artist's brush.

Mouse in the house

Uncoloured natural marzipan, made with egg whites, works best for marzipan shapes that you want to colour because it accepts colour readily.

MAKES 2

50g/2oz marzipan tinted as desired
small quantity royal icing

1 Take a 2.5cm/1in ball of coloured marzipan and roll it so that it is smooth. Hold the ball between the palms of both hands and gently put pressure on one end to form a cone shape.

2 For the ears, roll two tiny balls of marzipan completely smooth. Use a modelling tool to create the indent. Stick the ears to the sides of the head using water.

3 Make a round black nose. Create indents for the eyes and fill with icing blobs. Add black eyeballs. Paint on the eyebrows with food colouring. Model a black tail.

Spider in the web

It is difficult to tint marzipan black without changing the consistency of it, so for an intense shade buy ready coloured.

MAKES 2

50g/2oz black marzipan
small quantity icing
sprinkles

1 To make the web, cover the top of a cupcake with white glacé icing.

2 Pipe black circles with a fine plain nozzle on top. Starting at the centre and working to the edge, drag a cocktail stick (toothpick) through the lines of icing. Allow to set.

3 Form a smooth round head and a larger round body from marzipan using two balls of black marzipan. Dampen one side of one ball with water and stick the two balls together. Make indentations for the eyes.

4 Roll eight legs and stick under the body using water. Pipe white eyes in the sockets and a smiley mouth. Add black marzipan eyeballs, and sprinkles on the back.

Working with chocolate

Nearly everyone adores chocolate cakes, and chocolate is a rewarding and versatile decorating medium. It can be used to flavour buttercream and fudge icing, mixed with cream to make delectable ganache for fillings and toppings, or turned into crisp curls, leaves and other motifs.

Choosing chocolate for making ganache and truffles will be determined largely by the type you buy for eating. Purists who love 'real' chocolate with a high proportion of cocoa solids and an intense, bitter flavour will probably choose that for icings and fillings, while those with a sweet tooth who like to eat milk chocolate may prefer a dark chocolate with a lower cocoa content.

Plain (semisweet) chocolate contains about 30 per cent cocoa solids and is fairly sweet, with a pleasant chocolate flavour. It's good for making truffles, which can then be covered in a crisp coating of bitter chocolate to contrast with the soft, sweeter filling.

Dark (bittersweet) chocolate is sold in speciality shops and good supermarkets. It is more expensive and has a richer, more intense chocolate flavour. Look for a cocoa content of at least 70 per cent.

White chocolate contains only cocoa butter, milk solids and sugar. It is also fairly intolerant of heat, so always melt it carefully over warm water and watch it all the time. It will not set as solidly as dark chocolate when used as a coating.

Milk chocolate does not have such an intense chocolatey flavour as the dark chocolates. It contains a high proportion of milk solids, and for this reason it will not set as solidly as dark chocolate for a coating. This type of chocolate is best reserved for chocolate cake batters and icings.

Melting chocolate

Take special care when melting chocolate.

1 Break the chocolate into small pieces and put in a heatproof bowl over a pan of simmering water. Leave the chocolate for 1 minute then check it frequently – it may look solid when, in fact, it has melted.

Chocolate ganache

This amount of ganache is ample for coating the top of 25 cupcakes, or making 35 chocolate truffles.

150ml/¼ pint/⅔ cup double (heavy) cream
350g/12oz dark or plain (bitter- or semi-sweet) chocolate
50g/2oz/4 tbsp butter

1 Bring the cream to the boil. Remove from the heat and leave for 1 minute. Break the chocolate into the hot cream. Stir until the chocolate melts and the mixture is smooth.

2 Add the butter and continue to stir until the mixture looks glossy. Use it immediately for a topping. For truffles, chill, then scoop out balls. Toss in cocoa powder.

Right: Energy 115kcal/479kJ; Protein 0.7g; Carbohydrate 9.23g, of which sugars 8.5g; Fat 8.9g, of which saturates 5.2g; Cholesterol 14mg; Calcium 8mg; Fibre 0g; Sodium 19mg.

Chocolate curls

Arrange one or two of these lovely, fragile decorations on top of cakes iced with soft ganache or buttercream. Accomplishing perfect curls takes a little practice, but you can make them in advance and keep them in a sealed container in the refrigerator. Make plenty of spares as the crisp chocolate breaks easily.

1 Break dark chocolate into small pieces. Put in a heatproof bowl and melt over a pan of simmering water.

2 Using a round-bladed knife or the back of a spoon, spread the melted chocolate on to a marble slab, to a depth of about 6mm/¼in. Leave in a cool place to set.

3 Draw a long fine-bladed cook's knife across the chocolate at a 45 degree angle, using a see-saw action, to pare away long curls from the slab. If it becomes soft, chill it.

Chocolate leaves

These delicate leaves make a spectacular decoration for all kinds of cakes, especially if you make them using both dark and white chocolate. Rose leaves are an ideal shape and size, and the prominent veins on their undersides leave a perfect impression in the chocolate. Use an artist's brush to apply the chocolate as evenly as possible.

1 Break a slab of chocolate into small pieces. Put in a heatproof bowl and melt over a pan of simmering water.

2 Brush the chocolate evenly over the underside of clean, dry rose leaves. Put the leaves on a baking sheet lined with baking parchment.

3 Leave the baking sheet in a cool place until the chocolate has set. Carefully peel off each leaf and chill the chocolate leaves in an airtight container until needed.

Making simple cupcake desserts

Cupcakes are not just for tea: freshly baked, these delectable little sponge cakes are a perfect accompaniment to ice cream or fruit, and can be flavoured and decorated in a host of ways. Try drizzling them with tangy fruit syrups or liqueurs, and serve with lashings of whipped cream.

Chocolate cupcakes with ice cream

To assemble this simple dessert for six people you'll need six cupcakes made using either of the basic methods (replacing 15g/½oz/2 tbsp flour with the same quantity of cocoa powder), 60ml/4 tbsp Kirsch, six scoops of your favourite ice cream and some extra cocoa powder for dusting.

1 Cut each cupcake into horizontal slices and drizzle with Kirsch.

2 Sandwich the slices together with a scoop of ice cream and arrange on serving plates. Decorate with a dusting of cocoa powder. Serve with a few berries if you like.

Fresh fruit-topped cupcakes

Use summer fruits and a dusting of icing sugar to dress up basic cupcakes. This luxurious way to serve them means they'll go down well with adults as well as children. For six, you'll need 250ml/8fl oz/1 cup whipping cream, 175g/6oz mixed berries and a little icing (confectioners') sugar.

1 Scoop out a circle of sponge from the top of each cake using the point of a small sharp knife, and set the tops aside.

2 Whip the cream until stiff peaks form. Place a spoonful of cream in each sponge and top with fruit. Replace the lids at an angle and dust with icing sugar.

Frosted fruit topping

Add a pretty, delicate decoration to light airy sponge cakes of any size by topping them with clusters of small fruits, finely crusted with sugar. Use strawberries, seedless grapes, cherries, blueberries and jewel-red clusters of redcurrants for a pretty mixture: just choose a few perfect specimens of each, and include a few small leaves and stems for a natural look.

1 Rinse the fruit and leaves and pat them dry with kitchen paper, as any dampness will dissolve the sugar.

VARIATIONS
Wild strawberry leaves and their tiny scarlet fruits frosted with sugar make a natural and appealing decoration for small red berry cakes. Herb leaves such as marjoram and sweet scented geranium, or edible flowers, such as borage, can also be frosted; they look wonderful with sugar-coated blueberries, blackberries and grapes. Use whole leaves, or separate herbs with small leaves into tiny sprigs.

2 Lightly beat an egg white until it is frothy but not stiff. Using a small artist's brush, coat each fruit, plus the stems and leaves, with the beaten egg white.

3 Dredge the fruits with caster (superfine) sugar. Leave to dry on baking parchment in a warm dry place, and arrange on the cake just before serving.

Packaging and presentation

Have fun packaging and gift wrapping your favourite cakes. A single beautifully boxed cupcake makes a charming small gift for a friend, or you could pack a whole batch to give as favours at the end of a party. Cakes in decorated cups made from paper look lovely on a celebration table.

Paper cupcake and muffin cases, which are available in a wonderful assortment of colours and many patterns – flowery, stripy, dotty, with little red hearts or with fluffy chicks – are far too pretty to be hidden away in the back of a kitchen cupboard or drawer. Store them in a large glass jar; there are so many attractively decorated ones to choose from.

Don't forget the other cake accessories you might have collected: silver dragées, sugarpaste decorations, and coloured ribbons for gift wrapping your freshly baked creations. These, too, will look equally attractive presented in glass jars to decorate your kitchen. The sight of this ever-ready supply of baking accessories and cake decorations will also inspire you to bake more beautiful cakes more often for family and friends.

Patterned card cake cups

It can be fun to personalize your fresh muffins and cupcakes with attractive home-made paper cups that wrap around the paper case. Simply slot the cakes inside before you serve them.

You will need some coloured strips of decorative craft paper (or wallpaper that has the right thickness and flexibility), a selection of decorative standard weight papers, decorative craft paper and thin coloured ribbons.

Cut strips of craft paper 3–4cm/ 1¼–1½in wide and long enough to fit round the circumference of the cupcakes. Bend the strip into a circle and stick the ends together with

Left Sugar pink and yellow wrappers are the perfect paper cases in which to bake and make a gift of Easter-themed cupcakes.

Above A host of ready-cut paper motifs are available from craft suppliers, or you can cut out your own decorations to make the finishing touches for your card cake cups.

small strips of sticky tape to make the cake cup. Make sure it is just large enough to sit the cakes or muffins inside: you should still see a tiny margin of the frilly paper case above the top of the card, so make a trial one before cutting out all the strips. Cut a second, slightly narrower strip from decorative craft paper or coloured papers and stick it in place along the centre of the card strip. Finally, tie a length of thin coloured cord or ribbon around the waist of the paper cup, finishing with a bow at the front (with the join at the back). Or you can add small paper decorations: butterflies for summer cakes, rabbits for Easter, numbers for special birthdays, and white doves for wedding cupcakes make appropriate motifs.

Presentation boxes

For birthday party gifts and holiday treats display scrumptious cakes inside small clear plastic boxes. Add a gorgeous ribbon and a paper blossom to make your edible gifts more special. Plain card gift boxes in pretty colours turn a beautifully iced cupcake into a lovely gift. Choose colours and styles to suit your cakes (or choose the wrappings first and colour the icing and decorations to match your presentation theme). Line the box lavishly with tissue to keep your creations safe inside, and tie up the parcel with a length of satin ribbon and a pretty tag.

Below Tiny morsels of sweet cake are decorated with bright and colourful icing. Wrapped in pretty packaging, they make a delightful present just to say 'thank you'.

Above Fit two cupcakes in a larger box to make an indulgent present for two.
Below Iced and decorated cupcakes make appealing gifts.

Teatime treats

This delicious selection of cupcakes rings the changes on basic sponge cake recipes, and offers plenty of variety to inspire you, from luscious chocolate and spice cakes to summery fresh berry muffins and tangy citrus confections. Ingredients such as crunchy nuts, chocolate chips and fresh fruit mean that these little cakes don't need icing, though some are drizzled with simple glazes.

Espresso cupcakes with maple syrup

Strong dark coffee and maple syrup give a bitter edge to the sweetness of these little cakes. Drizzle more maple syrup over them while they are still warm. This recipe uses freshly made espresso, but you could use your own favourite coffee made at double strength.

MAKES 12

250g/9oz/2¼ cups plain
  (all-purpose) flour
10ml/2 tsp baking powder
pinch of cinnamon
50g/2oz/¼ cup golden caster
  (superfine) sugar
75g/3oz/6 tbsp butter
1 egg
105ml/7 tbsp pure maple syrup,
  plus extra for drizzling
105ml/7 tbsp strong coffee
45ml/3 tbsp buttermilk

1 Preheat the oven to 180°C/350°F/ Gas 4. Line a bun tin (pan) with paper cases. Sift the flour, baking powder and cinnamon into a large bowl and mix in the sugar.

2 Melt the butter, pour it into another mixing bowl and leave to cool. Beat the egg and stir it into the butter. Add the maple syrup, coffee and buttermilk.

3 Fold the egg mixture lightly into the dry ingredients until just combined. Spoon the mixture into the cases and bake for about 25 minutes. Serve with extra maple syrup drizzled over the top.

167kcal/703kJ; Protein 2.7g; Carbohydrate 27.6g, of which sugars 11.8g; Fat 5.9g, of which saturates 3.6g; Cholesterol 30mg; Calcium 42mg; Fibre 0.7g; Sodium 79mg.

Honey and spice cakes

These little golden cakes are fragrant with honey and cinnamon. Though their appearance is more traditional when they are cooked directly in a bun tin, they tend to rise higher and are therefore lighter when baked in paper cases.

MAKES 18

250g/9oz/2¼ cups plain (all-
 purpose) flour
5ml/1 tsp ground cinnamon
5ml/1 tsp bicarbonate of soda
 (baking soda)
125g/4½oz/½ cup butter,
 softened
125g/4½oz/10 tbsp soft dark
 brown sugar
1 egg, separated
125g/4½oz/10 tbsp clear honey
60ml/4 tbsp milk

1 Preheat the oven to 200°C/400°F/
Gas 6. Butter the cups of two bun
tins (pans) or line them with paper
cake cases.

2 Sift the flour into a large mixing
bowl, together with the ground
cinnamon and the bicarbonate
of soda.

3 Beat the butter with the sugar in
another large mixing bowl using an
electric mixer until the mixture is
very light and fluffy.

4 Beat in the egg yolk, then
gradually add the honey.

5 Lightly fold the flour, spice and
bicarbonate of soda into the mixture
until just combined.

6 Add sufficient milk from the
measured amount to make a soft
mixture that will just drop off the
spoon. Do not make the mixture too
wet or the cakes will be heavy.

7 In a separate bowl, whisk the
separated egg white until stiff peaks
form. Using a large metal spoon,
fold the egg white gently into the
cake mixture.

8 Divide the mixture among the tins
or cases. Bake for about 25 minutes,
until lightly coloured. Leave to stand
for 5 minutes before transferring to a
wire rack to cool.

Energy 152kcal/639kJ; Protein 1.9g; Carbohydrate 23.6g, of which sugars 13g; Fat 6.3g, of which saturates 3.8g; Cholesterol 26mg; Calcium 30mg; Fibre 0.4g; Sodium 49mg.

Chocolate chip cakes

Nothing could be easier – or nicer – than these classic muffins. The muffin mixture is plain, but has a surprise layer of chocolate chips inside. Sprinkle a few chocolate chips on top of the cakes to make them look irresistible. They are delicious eaten warm.

3 Sift the flour and baking powder together twice. Fold into the butter mixture, alternating with the milk.

4 Divide half the mixture among the paper cases. Sprinkle with half the chocolate chips, then cover with the remaining mixture and the rest of the chocolate chips. Bake for about 25 minutes, until golden. Leave to stand for 5 minutes then transfer to a wire rack to cool.

MAKES 10

115g/4oz/½ cup butter, softened
75g/3oz/⅓ cup caster (superfine) sugar
30ml/2 tbsp soft dark brown sugar
2 eggs
175g/6oz/1½ cups plain (all-purpose) flour
5ml/1 tsp baking powder
120ml/4fl oz/½ cup milk
175g/6oz/1 cup plain (semisweet) chocolate chips

1 Preheat the oven to 190°C/375°F/Gas 5. Arrange 10 paper cases in a muffin tin (pan).

2 In a large bowl, beat the butter until it is pale and light. Add the caster and dark brown sugars and beat until the mixture is light and fluffy. Beat in the eggs, one at a time, beating thoroughly after each addition.

Energy 296kcal/1241kJ; Protein 4.2g; Carbohydrate 36.5g, of which sugars 22.3g; Fat 15.9g, of which saturates 9.5g; Cholesterol 67mg; Calcium 59mg; Fibre 0.5g; Sodium 110mg.

Chunky chocolate and banana cupcakes

Luxurious but not overly sweet, these cakes are simple and quick to make. They taste best if served while still warm, when the chocolate is soft and gooey, but including bananas in the mixture gives a moist result and means the cakes will keep for a couple of days.

MAKES 12

90ml/6 tbsp semi-skimmed
  (low-fat) milk
2 eggs
150g/5oz/⅔ cup butter, melted
225g/8oz/2 cups plain (all-purpose)
  flour
5ml/1 tsp baking powder
150g/5oz/¾ cup golden caster
  (superfine) sugar
150g/5oz plain (semisweet)
  chocolate, cut into chunks
2 small bananas, mashed

3 Sift together the flour and baking powder into a separate bowl. Add the sugar, chocolate and bananas to the flour mixture.

4 Stir gently to combine, gradually stirring in the milk and egg mixture, but do not beat it. Spoon the mixture into the paper cases. Bake for about 20 minutes until the cakes are risen and golden. Allow to stand for 5 minutes, then turn out and leave to cool on a wire rack.

COOK'S TIP
Choose bananas that are fully ripe and can be mashed easily.

1 Preheat the oven to 200°C/400°F/ Gas 6. Arrange 12 paper cases in a muffin tin (pan).

2 In a small bowl, whisk the milk, eggs and melted butter together until combined.

Energy 303kcal/1268kJ; Protein 4g; Carbohydrate 40g, of which sugars 24.6g; Fat 15.2g, of which saturates 9.3g; Cholesterol 62mg; Calcium 54mg; Fibre 0.8g; Sodium 112mg.

Fresh raspberry and fig cakes

Beautiful purple figs, with their luscious red flesh, nestle with fresh raspberries in this delicious cake batter, which puffs up around them in a golden dome as it bakes. Cakes made with fresh summer fruit are a seasonal treat and best eaten while still warm from the oven.

MAKES 8–9

140g/5oz/¾ cup fresh raspberries
15ml/1 tbsp caster (superfine) sugar
3 fresh figs
225g/8oz/2 cups plain (all-purpose) flour
10ml/2 tsp baking powder
140g/5oz/¾ cup golden (superfine) caster sugar
85g/3½oz/7 tbsp butter, melted
1 egg, beaten
285ml/½ pint buttermilk
grated rind of ½ small orange

1 Preheat the oven to 180°C/350°F/ Gas 4. Grease the cups of a large muffin tin (pan) or line with paper muffin cases.

2 Arrange the fresh raspberries in a single layer on a large plate and sprinkle them evenly with the 15ml/ 1 tbsp caster sugar. Slice the figs vertically into eighths and set them aside with the raspberries.

3 Sift the flour and baking powder into a large mixing bowl and mix in the sugar. Make a well in the centre of the dry ingredients.

4 In another bowl, mix the cooled melted butter with the egg, butter-milk and grated orange rind. Pour this mixture into the dry ingredients and fold in gently until just blended. Do not overwork the mixture.

5 Set aside a small quantity of the raspberries and figs. Sprinkle the remaining fruit over the surface of the batter and fold in lightly. Spoon the mixture into the tin or the paper cases, filling each not more than two-thirds full.

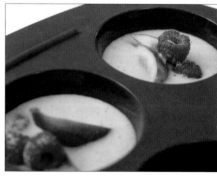

6 Lightly press the reserved fruit into the top of the batter. Bake for 22–25 minutes until the muffins are risen and golden. Leave in the tin for 5 minutes, then turn out on to a wire rack to cool, or serve while still warm as a dessert.

Energy 260kcal/1098kJ; Protein 4.7g; Carbohydrate 43.2g, of which sugars 24.2g; Fat 8.9g, of which saturates 5.4g; Cholesterol 44mg; Calcium 107mg; Fibre 1.7g; Sodium 102mg.

Raspberry crumble buns

Make these stylish cakes for a special meal in the summer when raspberries are bursting with flavour. For total luxury, serve like scones, with raspberry jam and cream. The nutty crumble topping contrasts beautifully with the soft fruit inside.

MAKES 12

175g/6oz/1½ cups plain (all-
   purpose) flour
10ml/2 tsp baking powder
5ml/1 tsp ground cinnamon
50g/2oz/¼ cup caster (superfine)
   sugar
50g/2oz/¼ cup soft light brown
   sugar
115g/4oz/½ cup butter, melted
1 egg
120ml/4fl oz/½ cup milk
225g/8oz/1⅓ cups fresh raspberries
grated rind of 1 lemon

For the crumble topping
50g/2oz/½ cup pecan nuts,
   finely chopped
50g/2oz/¼ cup soft dark
   brown sugar
45ml/3 tbsp plain (all-purpose)
   flour
5ml/1 tsp ground cinnamon
40g/1½oz/3 tbsp butter, melted

1 Preheat the oven to 180°C/350°F/ Gas 4. Arrange 12 paper cases in a muffin tin (pan).

2 Sift the flour, baking powder and cinnamon into a large bowl. Stir in the two kinds of sugar. Make a well in the centre.

3 In another bowl beat together the cooled, melted butter, egg and milk in another bowl until the mixture is smooth and light. Pour it into the well in the centre of the flour mixture and stir in gradually until just combined.

4 Stir in the raspberries and lemon rind. Spoon the batter into the muffin cases, filling them almost to the top.

5 To make the crumble topping, mix the pecans, sugar, flour and cinnamon in a large mixing bowl. Stir in the melted butter to create a crumbly texture.

6 Spoon a little of the crumble over the top of each muffin. Bake for about 25 minutes until they are risen and golden.

7 Leave to stand for 5 minutes, then transfer to a wire rack to cool slightly. Serve while still warm.

Energy 251kcal/1051kJ; Protein 3.4g; Carbohydrate 28.9g, of which sugars 14.9g; Fat 14.4g, of which saturates 7.5g; Cholesterol 46mg; Calcium 56mg; Fibre 1.2g; Sodium 110mg.

Citrus syrup cupcakes

These moist, syrupy cakes, with a very intense tangy citrus flavour, are made without flour, which makes them entirely safe to eat for anyone who has a wheat allergy. To make a luscious dessert add your choice of berries and a scoop of vanilla ice cream.

3 Remove the fruit from the water and leave to cool. Split open and discard the pips (seeds). Liquidize the fruit into a purée. Set aside.

4 Whisk the eggs and sugar together until foamy, then stir in the ground almonds and the fruit purée. Pour the mixture into the prepared cases and bake for 30 minutes.

5 To make the citrus syrup, dissolve the sugar in 250ml/9fl oz water over a medium heat. Add the strips of rind and the lemon juice and bring to the boil. Reduce the heat and simmer for 2–3 minutes, until the liquid coats the back of a spoon.

MAKES 12

3 clementines
6 eggs
225g/8oz/1 cup caster (superfine) sugar
225g/8oz/2 cups ground almonds
icing (confectioners') sugar, to dust

For the citrus syrup
350g/12oz/3 cups caster (superfine) sugar
rind of 1 clementine, pith removed, cut into very fine strips
juice of ¾ lemon

1 Put the whole, unpeeled clementines into a pan and cover generously with boiling water. Bring to the boil, then simmer for about 2 hours. This will soften the fruit and remove some of the bitterness from the skin. Keep a check on the water level and top up as necessary with boiling water.

2 Meanwhile, preheat the oven to 160°C/325°F/Gas 3. Set 12 oblong silicone cake cases on a baking sheet, or line a 12-hole bun tin (pan) with paper cake cases.

6 Allow the cakes to cool in the cases, then drizzle the warm syrup over, a spoonful at a time.

Energy 344kcal/1449kJ; Protein 7.4g; Carbohydrate 52.2g, of which sugars 51.7g; Fat 13.3g, of which saturates 1.7g; Cholesterol 95mg; Calcium 88mg; Fibre 1.5g; Sodium 41mg.

Orange cupcakes with orange glaze

These delicious cakes are ideal as a snack with a cup of tea or frothy cappuccino. They are finished with a slightly sour orange glaze that perfectly complements the sweetness of the cakes. If Seville oranges are not available you can use a mixture of sweet orange and lemon.

MAKES 9–10

75g/3oz/6 tbsp butter
1 egg, lightly beaten
175ml/6fl oz/¾ cup buttermilk
juice of 1½ Seville (Temple)
    oranges, plus grated rind of 2
    Seville oranges
225g/8oz/2 cups plain (all-purpose)
    flour
10ml/2 tsp baking powder
150g/5oz/¾ golden caster
    (superfine) sugar
15ml/1 tbsp Seville orange
    marmalade

For the orange glaze
juice and finely grated rind of
    ½ Seville (Temple) orange
75–90ml/5–6 tbsp icing
    (confectioners') sugar, sifted
5ml/1 tsp Seville orange
    marmalade

1 Preheat the oven to 180°C/350°F/ Gas 4. Lightly grease a muffin tin (pan). Melt the butter in a pan over a low heat, set aside to cool slightly.

2 In a bowl mix together the egg, buttermilk, orange juice and grated rind and the cooled, melted butter.

3 Add the flour, baking powder and sugar. Fold in gently, with the marmalade, until just blended.

4 Spoon the mixture into the tin, filling almost to the top. Bake for 25 minutes until golden. Leave to stand then turn on to a wire rack to cool.

5 To make the orange glaze, put the juice in a bowl and beat in the sugar, grated rind and marmalade. The mixture should cover the back of a spoon, but be thin and fluid. Drizzle the glaze in a loose zigzag over the tops of the cakes just before serving.

Energy 242kcal/1020kJ; Protein 3.5g; Carbohydrate 43.9g, of which sugars 26.8g; Fat 7g, of which saturates 4.3g; Cholesterol 37mg; Calcium 70mg; Fibre 0.7g; Sodium 76mg.

Blueberry buns

Light and fruity, these popular American muffins are delicious at any time of day. Serve them warm for breakfast or brunch, or as a teatime treat. Blueberries have a sweet but tangy flavour and are perfect for baking because they hold their shape during cooking.

MAKES 12

2 eggs
50g/2oz/4 tbsp butter, melted
175ml/6fl oz/¾ cup milk
5ml/1 tsp vanilla extract
5ml/1 tsp grated lemon rind

175g/6oz/1½ cups plain (all-purpose) flour
50g/2oz/¼ cup caster (superfine) sugar
10ml/2 tsp baking powder
175g/6oz/1½ cups blueberries

1 Preheat the oven to 200°C/400°F/Gas 6. Arrange 12 paper cases in a muffin tin (pan) or grease the tin.

2 Whisk the eggs until blended and stir in the melted butter, milk, vanilla and lemon rind.

3 Sift the flour, sugar and baking powder into another large bowl. Make a well in the centre and add the egg mixture. Stir in lightly with a metal spoon.

4 Fold in the blueberries gently, then spoon the batter into the muffin tin or paper cases.

5 Bake for 20–25 minutes, until the tops spring back when touched lightly. Leave in the tin for 5 minutes before turning out on to a wire rack.

Energy 236kcal/992kJ; Protein 4.9g; Carbohydrate 34.7g, of which sugars 12.4g; Fat 9.6g, of which saturates 5.6g; Cholesterol 54mg; Calcium 88mg; Fibre 1.4g; Sodium 82mg.

Apple and Calvados cakes

The subtle bouquet of Calvados (Normandy apple brandy) and the earthy, fruity flavour of quince add depth to simple apple cakes. Quince paste is always available, but when the fruit is in season replace a third of the chopped apple with finely grated fresh quince to add extra flavour.

MAKES 10

250g/9oz cooking apple, peeled
  and cored
grated rind of 1 lemon
45ml/3 tbsp quince paste
75g/3oz/6 tbsp butter, melted
15ml/1 tbsp Calvados
225g/8oz/2 cups plain
  (all-purpose) flour
10ml/2 tsp baking powder
75g/3oz/⅓ cup caster
  (superfine) sugar
1 egg, lightly beaten
60ml/4 tbsp buttermilk

For the quince glaze
45ml/3 tbsp quince or apple jelly
15ml/1 tbsp water
5ml/1 tsp lemon juice
30ml/2 tbsp Calvados

1 Preheat the oven to 180°C/350°F/ Gas 4. Grease the cups of a large muffin tin (pan) or line them with paper muffin cases.

2 Slice one quarter of the apple very thinly and reserve in a bowl of water acidulated with a squeeze of lemon. Roughly dice the rest of the apple and set aside in another bowl of acidulated water.

3 In a small pan, gently melt the quince paste with the butter over a low heat, mashing the paste with a wooden spoon to break up any little lumps.

4 Remove the pan from the heat. Stir in the Calvados and set aside.

5 Sift the dry ingredients into a large bowl. In another bowl, stir the egg and the buttermilk together and add the grated lemon rind.

6 Pour the egg mixture into the dry ingredients, with the butter, quince paste and Calvados and the chopped apple. Stir until just combined, then spoon into the prepared muffin tin.

7 Press a few slices of apple into the top of each cake. Bake for 25–30 minutes until golden.

8 To make the glaze, put the jelly, water and lemon juice in a small pan, and boil rapidly until slightly thickened. Add the Calvados and simmer for about 1 minute. Brush over the muffins while still warm.

Energy 213kcal/899kJ; Protein 3.1g; Carbohydrate 34.1g, of which sugars 16.9g; Fat 7.1g, of which saturates 4.3g; Cholesterol 37mg; Calcium 50mg; Fibre 1.1g; Sodium 70mg.

Nutty cakes with walnut liqueur

These spicy little cakes have a crunchy topping and moist crumb studded with chopped walnuts: chop the nuts very coarsely to give the cakes plenty of texture. The walnut liqueur brings out their flavour and adds a little punch and warmth of its own.

2 Sift the flour, baking powder and mixed spice into a large bowl. Stir in the sugar and the chopped walnuts, reserving about 15ml/ 1 tbsp of each to sprinkle over the top of the cakes. Make a well in the centre.

3 Pour the butter mixture into the dry ingredients and stir for just long enough to combine the ingredients. Do not overmix: the nuts mean that the batter will be lumpy.

4 Fill the paper muffin cases two-thirds full, then top with a sprinkling of the reserved sugar and walnuts. Bake for about 15 mintues until the muffins have risen and are golden brown. Leave to stand for about 5 minutes, then turn out on to a wire rack to cool.

MAKES 12

50g/2oz/4 tbsp butter, melted
2 eggs, beaten
175ml/6fl oz/³⁄₄ cup milk
30ml/2 tbsp walnut liqueur
225g/8oz/2 cups plain
  (all-purpose) flour
20ml/4 tsp baking powder
2.5ml/¹⁄₂ tsp mixed (apple
  pie) spice
115g/4oz/²⁄₃ cup soft light
  brown sugar
75g/3oz/³⁄₄ cup chopped walnuts

1 Preheat the oven to 200°C/400°F/ Gas 6. Line a muffin tin (pan) with paper cases. In a jug (pitcher) mix the butter, eggs, milk and liqueur.

Energy 201kcal/844kJ; Protein 4.3g; Carbohydrate 26.3g, of which sugars 12g; Fat 9.1g, of which saturates 3g; Cholesterol 42mg; Calcium 60mg; Fibre 0.8g; Sodium 53mg.

Gooey butterscotch cakes

If you like, you can make up the two mixtures for these cakes the night before you need them and stir them together first thing next day for an irresistible mid-morning treat. Instead of butterscotch, you could try adding chocolate chips, marshmallows or blueberries.

MAKES 9–12

150g/5oz butterscotch sweets
  (candies)
225g/8oz/2 cups plain
  (all purpose) flour
90g/3½oz/½ cup golden caster
  (superfine) sugar
10ml/2 tsp baking powder
pinch of salt
1 egg, beaten
150ml/¼ pint/⅔ cup milk
50ml/2fl oz/¼ cup sunflower oil or
  melted butter
75g/3oz/¾ cup chopped hazelnuts

1 Preheat the oven to 200°C/400°F/
Gas 6. Arrange 9–12 paper cases in
a muffin tin (pan).

2 With floured fingers, break the
butterscotch sweets into small
chunks. Toss them in a little flour,
if necessary, to prevent them from
sticking together.

3 Sift together the flour, sugar,
baking powder and salt into a large
mixing bowl.

4 Whisk together the egg, milk and
oil or melted butter, then stir the
mixture into the dry ingredients
with the sweets and nuts. Stir
together only lightly – the mixture
should be lumpy.

5 Spoon the batter evenly into the
paper cases, filling about half full.
Bake for 20 minutes, until risen and
golden. They should spring back
when pressed lightly in the centre.

6 Leave the muffins in the tin for
5 minutes, then remove and transfer
to a wire rack to cool.

COOK'S TIP
Try drizzling these muffins with
the Spanish treat dulce de leche
– a thick caramelized syrup.

Energy 224kcal/941kJ; Protein 3.9g; Carbohydrate 31.7g, of which sugars 14.6g; Fat 10g, of which saturates 2.1g; Cholesterol 19mg; Calcium 66mg; Fibre 1g; Sodium 55mg.

Lemon meringue cakes

This recipe is a delightful amalgam of a traditional fairy cake with the classic lemon meringue pie – soft lemon sponge cake is topped with crisp meringue. The little cakes are lovely with tea, but can also be served hot as a dessert, accompanied by cream or ice cream.

MAKES 18

115g/4oz/½ cup butter, softened
200g/7oz/scant 1 cup caster (superfine) sugar
2 eggs
115g/4oz/1 cup self-raising (self-rising) flour
5ml/1 tsp baking powder
grated rind of 2 lemons
30ml/2 tbsp lemon juice
2 egg whites

1 Preheat the oven to 190ºC/375ºF/ Gas 5. Arrange 18 paper cases in muffin tins (pans).

2 Put the butter in a bowl and beat until soft. Add 115g/4oz/generous ½ cup of the caster sugar and continue to beat until the mixture is light and creamy. Add the eggs, one at a time, beating thoroughly after each addition until the mixture is smooth.

3 Sift together the flour and baking powder over the creamed mixture, add half the lemon rind and all the lemon juice and beat well until thoroughly combined.

4 Divide the mixture among the paper cases, filling each case about two-thirds full.

5 To make the meringue, whisk the egg whites in a clean grease-free bowl until they stand in soft peaks. Stir in the remaining caster sugar and lemon rind.

6 Put a spoonful of the meringue mixture on top of each cake. Cook for 20–25 minutes, until the meringue is crisp and brown. Serve the cakes hot or turn out on to a wire rack to cool.

Energy 123kcal/514kJ; Protein 1.7g; Carbohydrate 16.6g, of which sugars 11.7g; Fat 6g, of which saturates 3.5g; Cholesterol 35mg; Calcium 19mg; Fibre 0.2g; Sodium 54mg.

Mandarin syrup cupcakes

For this recipe, mandarins are boiled to soften them and remove some of the bitterness, then puréed to add an intense citrus flavour to the finished cakes, which are then saturated in a citrus syrup. Serve as cakes or as a sumptuous dessert with a compote of fresh fruit.

MAKES 12

3 mandarins
225g/8oz caster (superfine) sugar
6 medium (US large) eggs
225g/8oz ground almonds

For the syrup
350g/12oz caster (superfine) sugar
zest of 2 mandarins cut into very
   fine strips
juice of ¾ lemon

1 Preheat the oven to 160°C/325°F/ Gas 3. Line a 12-hole muffin tin (pan) with paper cases.

2 Put the whole unpeeled mandarins into a pan and cover generously with boiling water. Bring to the boil then simmer for about 2 hours. Keep a check on the water level and top up if necessary.

3 Remove the mandarins from the water and when the fruit has cooled, split open and remove the pips. Liquidize them into a smooth orange purée and set aside.

4 Whisk the eggs and sugar until well combined.

5 Stir in the ground almonds and the puréed fruit.

6 Spoon the mixture into the prepared cases and bake for 30 minutes until golden.

7 To make the syrup, dissolve the sugar over a medium heat in 250ml/ 9fl oz water. Add the strips of fruit zest and the lemon juice and bring to the boil. Simmer for 2–3 minutes. Spoon on to the surface of the cakes.

Energy 344kcal/1449kJ; Protein 7.4g; Carbohydrate 52.2g, of which sugars 51.7g; Fat 13.3g, of which saturates 1.7g; Cholesterol 95mg; Calcium 88mg; Fibre 1.5g; Sodium 41mg.

Chocolate and sour cherry cakes

Sour cherries have an intense, tangy flavour, a contrast to the sweetness of white chocolate. These muffins, made with pure extracts of chocolate and vanilla, are topped with a vibrantly fruity sour cherry and white chocolate icing.

1 Preheat the oven to 180°C/350°F/ Gas 4. Grease the cups of a large muffin tin (pan). Sift the flour, baking powder and salt into a large mixing bowl and mix in the sugar. Set aside.

2 In a pan melt the butter, then remove it from the heat. Break half the chocolate into the melted butter and stir until melted. Grate the remaining chocolate and set aside.

3 In a bowl, whisk together the egg, milk, vanilla and chocolate extracts. Stir into the dry ingredients with the melted chocolate butter and the grated chocolate. Fold the ingredients lightly together.

4 Divide the batter among the muffin cups, filling three-quarters full. Bake for 25 minutes until golden. Turn on to a rack to cool.

5 To make the icing, melt the white chocolate in a bowl set over a pan of gently simmering water. Stir in the icing sugar and the butter. Add 15ml/1 tbsp warm water and mix until smooth. Add the dried fruit. Coat the tops of the cooled muffins.

MAKES 10

225g/8oz/2 cups plain (all-purpose) flour
10ml/2 tsp baking powder
pinch of salt
75g/3oz/⅓ cup golden caster (superfine) sugar
75g/3oz/6 tbsp butter
130g/4½oz milk chocolate
1 small (US medium) egg, lightly beaten

90ml/6 tbsp milk
5ml/1 tsp vanilla extract
5ml/1 tsp pure chocolate extract

For the white chocolate and sour cherry icing
100g/3½oz vanilla white chocolate
50g/2oz/½ cup icing (confectioners') sugar, sifted
40g/1½oz butter
40g/1½oz dried sour cherries, roughly chopped

Energy 369kcal/1546kJ; Protein 5.1g; Carbohydrate 47.2g, of which sugars 29.7g; Fat 19.1g, of which saturates 11.7g; Cholesterol 55mg; Calcium 112mg; Fibre 0.7g; Sodium 142mg.

Blueberry and chocolate cupcakes

Blueberries are one of the many fruits that combine deliciously with the richness of chocolate in cakes, while still retaining their own distinctive flavour. These cakes are best served on the day they are made, preferably while still warm.

MAKES 12

115g/4oz/½ cup butter
75g/3oz plain (semisweet)
  chocolate, chopped
200g/7oz/scant 1 cup sugar
1 egg, lightly beaten
250ml/8fl oz/1 cup buttermilk
10ml/2 tsp vanilla extract
275g/10oz/2½ cups plain (all-
  purpose) flour
5ml/1 tsp bicarbonate of soda
  (baking soda)
175g/6oz/generous 1 cup fresh or
  thawed frozen blueberries
25g/1oz plain (semisweet)
  chocolate, melted, to decorate

1 Preheat the oven to 190°C/375°F/ Gas 5. Arrange 12 paper cases in a muffin tin (pan).

2 Melt the butter and chocolate in a pan over a medium heat, stirring frequently, until smooth. Remove from the heat and leave the mixture to cool slightly.

3 Put the sugar in a mixing bowl, add the egg, buttermilk and vanilla extract, and pour in the chocolate mixture. Stir until smooth.

4 Sift the flour and bicarbonate of soda over the mixture, then gently fold in until just blended. (The mixture should be slightly lumpy.)

5 Gently fold in the blueberries. Spoon the batter into the paper cases. Bake for 25–30 minutes, until a skewer inserted in the centre comes out with just a few crumbs attached. Remove from the oven and leave in the tin for 5 minutes, then turn the muffins out on to a wire rack to cool.

6 If serving warm, drizzle melted chocolate over the top of each, then serve. Otherwise, leave until cold before decorating.

Energy 203kcal/850kJ; Protein 3.9g; Carbohydrate 24.9g, of which sugars 6.6g; Fat 10.5g, of which saturates 6.4g; Cholesterol 39mg; Calcium 63mg; Fibre 1g; Sodium 90mg.

Raspberry crunch friands

In this recipe egg whites are combined with ground nuts, melted butter and very little flour. The raw mixture has quite a loose consistency, but don't worry – as the cakes bake they will become just as firm and well risen as other cakes with a higher proportion of flour.

MAKES 12

175g/6oz/¾ cup butter
115g/4oz/1 cup ground almonds
225g/8oz/2 cups icing (confectioners') sugar, sifted
70g/2½oz/9 tbsp plain (all-purpose) flour, sifted
6 egg whites
115g/4oz/¾ cup fresh raspberries

For the crunchy sugar frosting
juice of 1 small lemon
150g/5oz/¾ cup caster (superfine) sugar
very finely cut strips of candied lemon rind (optional)

1 Preheat the oven to 200°C/400°F/Gas 6. Grease the cups of a friand or bun tin (pan) with melted butter and dust lightly with flour. Turn the tin upside down and tap it sharply on the work surface to get rid of any excess flour.

2 Melt the butter, remove from the heat and set aside to cool slightly.

3 Put the ground almonds, sugar and flour in a mixing bowl and stir together.

4 In a separate bowl, beat the egg whites lightly for 15 seconds, or just enough to break them up.

5 Add the egg whites to the dry ingredients and mix. Add the melted butter to the bowl and mix lightly until just combined.

6 Pour the mixture into the cups and press one raspberry into the centre of each. Bake for 20–25 minutes until the friands are pale golden and springy to the touch. Leave to cool slightly then turn them out on to a wire rack.

7 To make the sugar frosting, mix the lemon juice with the sugar and set aside for 10 minutes for the sugar to partly dissolve. Drizzle over the tops of the cooled cakes and leave to set for several hours. Top with a few curls of candied lemon rind, if you like.

Energy 317kcal/1330kJ; Protein 4.4g; Carbohydrate 38.3g, of which sugars 33.6g; Fat 17.4g, of which saturates 8.4g; Cholesterol 34mg; Calcium 53mg; Fibre 1.1g; Sodium 143mg.

Little Madeira cakes with cream and jam

This recipe looks as good as it tastes. The Madeira cake mixture, enriched with ground almonds and Calvados, rises beautifully into a perfect dome. When the cakes have cooled the domes are carefully sliced away to make room for a mouthwatering filling of buttercream and raspberry jam.

MAKES 14

225g/8oz/1 cup butter, softened
225g/8oz/1 cup caster
  (superfine) sugar
4 eggs
225g/8oz/2 cups self-raising (self-
  rising) flour
115g/4oz/1 cup plain (all-purpose)
  flour
60ml/4 tbsp ground almonds
5ml/1 tsp finely grated lemon rind
30ml/2 tbsp Calvados, brandy
  or milk

For the filling
175g/6oz/¾ cup butter, softened
350g/12oz/3 cups icing
  (confectioners') sugar, double
  sifted, plus extra for dusting
20ml/4 tsp lemon juice
20ml/4 tsp warm water
60ml/4 tbsp raspberry jam

1 Preheat the oven to 180°C/350°F/ Gas 4. Line 14 cups of two muffin tins (pans) with paper cases.

2 Cream the butter and caster sugar together until light and fluffy.

3 Add two of the eggs, a little at a time, mixing well after each addition. Sprinkle 15ml/1 tbsp of the flour into the mixture and beat it in. Add the remaining eggs gradually, beating well after each addition, then beat in another 15ml/1 tbsp flour until just combined. Sift the remaining flours into the mixture and fold in lightly with the ground almonds, lemon rind and Calvados, brandy or milk.

4 Fill the prepared cups almost to the top. Bake for 20–22 minutes until the tops spring back when touched and the cakes are light golden. Transfer to a wire rack.

5 To make the buttercream, beat the softened butter with the icing sugar until it is smooth and fluffy. Stir in the lemon juice and warm water and continue to beat until smooth.

6 When the cakes have cooled completely, slice a round from the top of each.

7 Using a large piping (pastry) bag fitted with a plain nozzle, pipe a circle of buttercream.

8 Add a spoonful of jam to fill each cake before replacing the dome on top. Just before serving, dust lightly with sifted icing sugar.

Energy 574kcal/2406kJ; Protein 5.2g; Carbohydrate 75.5g, of which sugars 54g; Fat 29.5g, of which saturates 18.6g; Cholesterol 140mg; Calcium 81mg; Fibre 0.9g; Sodium 278mg.

Simple decorations

The cupcakes in this chapter are prettily dressed up and perfect for a party table or a special tea. All the decorative ideas shown here are easy to achieve – from a light but stylish dusting of sugar to impressive swirls of chocolate or chestnut cream or beautifully moulded marzipan leaves – and the cupcakes underneath taste delicious too.

Chocolate fairy cakes

These magical little treats are sure to enchant adults and children alike. The chocolate sponge is rich, moist and dark, and contrasts appetizingly with the pure white vanilla-flavoured buttercream, which is swirled generously over the top.

MAKES 24

175g/6oz/¾ cup butter, softened
150ml/¼ pint/⅔ cup milk
5ml/1 tsp vanilla extract
115g/4oz plain (semisweet)
  chocolate, broken into pieces
15ml/1 tbsp water
275g/10oz/2½ cups plain (all-
  purpose) flour
5ml/1 tsp baking powder
2.5ml/½ tsp bicarbonate of soda
  (baking soda)
300g/11oz/1½ cups caster
  (superfine) sugar
3 eggs

For the vanilla icing
40g/1½oz/3 tbsp butter
115g/4oz/1 cup icing
  (confectioners') sugar
2.5ml/½ tsp vanilla
  extract
15–30ml/1–2 tbsp milk

1 Preheat the oven to 180°C/350°F/ Gas 4. Arrange 24 paper cases in muffin tins (pans), or grease the cups of the tins.

2 In a large mixing bowl, beat the butter with an electric mixer until it is light and fluffy. Beat in the milk and the vanilla extract.

3 Melt the chocolate with the water in a heatproof bowl set over a pan of simmering water, then add to the butter mixture.

4 Sift the flour, baking powder, bicarbonate of soda and sugar over the batter in batches and stir in. Add the eggs, one at a time; beat well after each addition.

5 Divide the mixture evenly among the muffin cases. Bake for 20–25 minutes or until a skewer inserted into the centre comes out clean. Turn out to cool on a wire rack.

6 To make the icing, beat the butter with the icing sugar and vanilla extract. Add just enough milk to make a creamy mixture. Spread on top of the cooled cakes.

Energy 210kcal/884kJ; Protein 2.5g; Carbohydrate 30.4g, of which sugars 21.6g; Fat 9.7g, of which saturates 5.8g; Cholesterol 44mg; Calcium 39mg; Fibre 0.5g; Sodium 67mg.

Soft cheese cupcakes

Although cupcakes are very popular nowadays, it's unusual to come across one with a mild goat's cheese flavour. A fresh flower decoration looks lovely, particularly if you have fresh pansies or purple violets at hand to press into the delicious sweet soft cheese frosting.

MAKES 12

140g/5oz/²⁄₃ cup butter, softened
185g/6½oz/¾ cup caster
  (superfine) sugar
3 eggs
15ml/1 tbsp grated lemon rind
140g/5oz/²⁄₃ cup soft goat's cheese
45ml/3 tbsp mixed (candied) peel,
  chopped
20ml/4 tsp buttermilk
200g/7oz/1¾ cups self-raising
  (self-rising) flour

For the frosting
450g/1lb/2 cups soft goat's cheese
300g/11oz/2¾ cups icing
  (confectioners') sugar, sifted
fresh edible flowers such as violets
  or pansies, to decorate

1 Preheat the oven to 180°C/350°F/ Gas 4. Line the cups of a bun tin (pan) with paper cases.

2 Beat the butter and caster sugar together until light and creamy. Gradually beat in the eggs, one at a time, beating well after each addition. Beat in the lemon rind, goat's cheese, mixed peel and buttermilk. Lightly fold in the flour.

3 Spoon the cake mixture into the prepared cups and lightly smooth it level. Bake for 25 minutes, or until the centre of the cake is firm and slightly springy to the touch. Leave to cool slightly, then turn out on to a wire rack to cool completely.

4 To make the frosting, soften the goat's cheese by beating it in a large mixing bowl. Stir in the sifted icing sugar until combined. Spread on top of the cooled cupcakes and decorate with edible flowers.

Energy 487kcal/2044kJ; Protein 13.8g; Carbohydrate 58g, of which sugars 45.3g; Fat 23.9g, of which saturates 15.5g; Cholesterol 120mg; Calcium 126mg; Fibre 0.7g; Sodium 415mg.

Simple cupcakes

These no-fuss cupcakes are perfect for a children's party, and the recipe is easy enough for the children to help you make them. The simple glacé icing is mixed with lemon juice for a tangy flavour; make small batches in different pastel colours if you like, for a pretty effect.

5 Fill the prepared cups half full. Bake for 13–15 minutes until the cakes look golden and the tops spring back when touched. Transfer to a wire rack to cool completely.

6 To make the icing, sift the icing sugar and gradually mix in the lemon juice and water until the mixture is smooth. Spoon a little icing on to each cake and smooth it level with a metal spatula.

ROSE PINK ICING
Place 175g/6oz/1½ cups sifted icing (confectioners') sugar in a bowl and mix with 5ml/1 tsp rose water and 25ml/5 tsp hot water until smooth. Mix in a few drops of pink food colouring.

MAKES 12

115g/4oz/1 cup self-raising (self-rising) flour
2.5ml/½ tsp baking powder
115g/4oz/½ cup butter, softened
115g/4oz/½ cup caster (superfine) sugar
2 eggs
5ml/1 tsp lemon juice

For the lemon icing
175g/6oz/1½ cups icing (confectioners') sugar
30ml/2 tbsp lemon juice
5ml/1 tsp hot water

1 Preheat the oven to 180°C/350°F/Gas 4. Line a 12-cup bun tin (pan) with paper cases.

2 Sift the flour with the baking powder and set aside.

3 In a large mixing bowl, beat the butter and sugar together using an electric mixer until light and fluffy.

4 Add the eggs a little at a time, beating the mixture well after each addition. Gently fold in the sifted flour using a metal spoon. Add the lemon juice and stir to blend.

Energy 211kcal/887kJ; Protein 2.1g; Carbohydrate 32.7g, of which sugars 25.4g; Fat 8.9g, of which saturates 5.5g; Cholesterol 54mg; Calcium 32mg; Fibre 0.3g; Sodium 85mg.

Lemon cupcakes with citrus crème fraîche

Add a zing to the afternoon break with the freshly baked aromas of lemon and cardamom – the signature ingredients in these delicious cupcakes. The lemony icing is made with tangy crème fraîche, and little sugarpaste flowers provide a simple finishing touch.

MAKES 8–9

225g/8oz/2 cups plain (all-purpose)
  flour
10ml/2 tsp baking powder
150g/5oz/¾ cup caster (superfine)
  sugar, or 75ml/5 tbsp
  clear honey
1 egg, beaten
300ml/½ pint/1¼ cups natural
  (plain) yogurt
15ml/1 tbsp freshly grated
  lemon rind
75g/3oz/6 tbsp butter, melted
8 cardamom seeds crushed to
  a powder

For the frosting and decoration
225g/8oz/1 cup crème fraîche
50g/2oz/½ cup icing
  (confectioners') sugar, double
  sifted, plus extra for dusting
juice of 1 lemon
finely grated rind of 2 lemons
small quantity of sugarpaste
paste food colouring

1 Preheat the oven to 180°C/350°F/ Gas 4. Line the cups of a bun tin (pan) with paper cases.

2 Sift the flour and baking powder into a large bowl and stir in the sugar (but not the honey, if using).

3 In another bowl mix together the egg, yogurt, lemon rind, honey (if using) and melted butter.

4 Add to the dry ingredients with the ground cardamom and fold lightly together until just mixed.

5 Spoon the mixture into the cases, filling them two-thirds full. Bake for 25 minutes until springy to the touch. Leave to cool on a wire rack.

6 To make the frosting, using an electric mixer whisk the crème fraîche, sugar, lemon juice and rind together for about 3 minutes until thick and creamy. Cover and chill for at least an hour.

7 Spread the frosting over the tops of the cooled cakes.

8 Tint the sugarpaste to the desired colour. Roll out to a thickness of 3mm/⅛in on a work surface dusted with sifted icing sugar and stamp a flower for each cake. Press a small ball of paste into each centre and shape the petals gently. Press a flower into the top of each cake.

Energy 238kcal/1004kJ; Protein 4.8g; Carbohydrate 39.2g, of which sugars 20.2g; Fat 8.1g, of which saturates 4.9g; Cholesterol 41mg; Calcium 108mg; Fibre 0.8g; Sodium 98mg.

Chocolate truffle cupcakes with Indian spices

These rich chocolate cakes, which have a fairly dense crumb, are lightly fragranced with warming Indian spices and topped generously with a smooth, buttery chocolate truffle mixture. Make them for a special Easter party and wait for the compliments.

MAKES 20

150g/5oz dark (bittersweet) chocolate, broken up
250ml/8fl oz/1 cup single (light) cream
5ml/1 tsp vanilla extract
2.5ml/½ tsp ground cinnamon
5ml/1 tsp ground cardamom
225g/8oz/1 cup caster (superfine) sugar
200g/7oz/scant 1 cup butter
3 eggs, separated
225g/8oz/2 cups plain (all-purpose) flour
20g/¾oz/3 tbsp unsweetened cocoa powder, plus extra for dusting
10ml/2 tsp baking powder
1 quantity chocolate ganache (see page 28) and truffles, to decorate

1 Preheat the oven to 180°C/350°F/Gas 4. Line the cups of two large bun tins (pans) with paper cases.

2 Put the chocolate and cream in a bowl set over a pan of simmering water. Stir continuously until the chocolate has melted and the mixture is smooth. Stir in the vanilla and spices and set aside.

3 Beat the sugar and butter together until light and fluffy, then gradually beat in the egg yolks one at a time.

4 Put the egg whites in a dry, clean bowl and whisk them until they form stiff peaks. Set aside.

5 Sift the flour, cocoa powder and baking powder together and fold into the butter and sugar mixture, alternately with the spiced chocolate cream, until evenly combined. (Do not overmix – the batter should be slightly lumpy.) Fold the egg whites lightly into the mixture using a metal spoon.

6 Spoon into the prepared cases and smooth the tops level. Bake for 20 minutes until the cakes are firm to the touch. Leave them in the tins for 5 minutes then turn out on to a wire rack to cool completely.

7 Ice the cakes with chocolate ganache, smoothing it with a metal spatula. Press cocoa-dusted truffles on to the top of each cake, and dust with a little extra sifted cocoa powder. Serve the cakes on the day of making.

Energy 380kcal/1587kJ; Protein 4g; Carbohydrate 37.6g, of which sugars 27.5g; Fat 25.2g, of which saturates 15.2g; Cholesterol 76mg; Calcium 54mg; Fibre 0.5g; Sodium 131mg.

Chocolate mint-filled cupcakes

These dark chocolate cakes have a sensational surprise inside: a luscious mint cream filling. For even more mint flavour, you could try chopping eight mint cream-filled dark chocolates and folding them into the cake batter just before filling the cases.

MAKES 12

150g/5oz/⅔ cup unsalted (sweet)
 butter, softened
300g/11oz/1½ cups caster
 (superfine) sugar
3 eggs
250ml/8fl oz/1 cup milk
5ml/1 tsp peppermint extract
225g/8oz/2 cups plain (all-purpose)
 flour
pinch of salt
5ml/1 tsp bicarbonate of soda
 (baking soda)
50g/2oz/½ cup unsweetened
 cocoa powder

For the filling
300ml/10fl oz/1¼ cups double
 (heavy) or whipping cream
5ml/1 tsp peppermint extract

For the topping
175g/6oz plain (semisweet)
 chocolate
115g/4oz/½ cup butter
5ml/1 tsp peppermint extract

1 Preheat the oven to 180°C/350°F/ Gas 4. Arrange 12 paper cases in a bun tin (pan).

2 Beat together the butter and sugar until creamy. Beat in the eggs, milk and peppermint. Sift the flour, salt, bicarbonate of soda and cocoa powder over the batter and mix in.

3 Fill the cases with the batter. Bake for 12–15 minutes, until a skewer inserted into the centre comes out clean. Cool on a wire rack.

4 To make the filling, whip the cream with the peppermint extract until it holds its shape. Spoon into a piping (pastry) bag fitted with a plain nozzle. Pipe about 15ml/1 tbsp into the centre of each muffin.

5 To make the topping, in a pan over a low heat melt the chocolate and butter. Remove from the heat and stir in the peppermint extract. Leave to cool, then spread on top of each cupcake.

Energy 555kcal/2315kJ; Protein 6.1g; Carbohydrate 52.3g, of which sugars 36.8g; Fat 38.6g, of which saturates 23.1g; Cholesterol 133mg; Calcium 98mg; Fibre 1.1g; Sodium 247mg.

Madeleine cakes with raspberry buttercream

These madeleine-style cupcakes have a gorgeous pink crumb and little shell-shaped decorations made from the same mixture, pressed over a glamorous pink swirl of raspberry buttercream. You will need a mini madeleine mould for the cake decorations, as well as a muffin tin for the cakes.

MAKES 9

115g/4oz/1 cup self-raising (self-rising) flour
100g/3½oz/scant ½ cup caster (superfine) sugar
115g/4oz/½ cup butter
3 eggs
50g/2oz/½ cup ground almonds
5ml/1 tsp rose water
9–12 drops red food colouring (optional)
½ quantity raspberry buttercream (see page 21), to decorate
sifted icing (confectioners') sugar, to dust

1 Preheat the oven to 190°C/375°F/Gas 5. Line nine cups of a muffin tin (pan) with paper cases and brush a mini madeleine mould with a little melted butter.

2 Sift the flour and salt into a bowl and stir in the sugar.

3 Melt the butter and leave to cool. Lightly beat the eggs and mix them into the sugar and flour, then add the cooled butter, ground almonds and rose water. Add the food colour if using. Mix well. Cover and chill for 1 hour. Fill the paper cases three-quarters full.

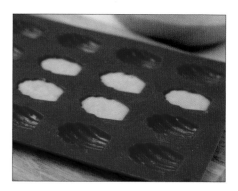

4 Half-fill the mini madeleine mould with mixture. Bake for 5–6 minutes, until golden. Bake the cakes for 20 minutes until well risen and firm to the touch. Leave to cool then turn out on to a wire rack.

5 When the cakes are cool, fill a large piping (pastry) bag fitted with a star nozzle with raspberry buttercream. Pipe a whirl over the centre of each cake and press a madeleine lightly to one side of it.

VARIATION
A little fresh raspberry juice, made by pressing the fresh fruit through a fine sieve, could be substituted for the food colour and adds extra flavour too.

Energy 364kcal/1523kJ; Protein 4.7g; Carbohydrate 39.3g, of which sugars 29.4g; Fat 22.1g, of which saturates 12g; Cholesterol 111mg; Calcium 58mg; Fibre 0.8g; Sodium 182mg.

Ginger cupcakes with lemon glacé icing

Cool lemon icing offsets the warm ginger flavour of these delicious little cakes, which are charmingly decorated with small 'gingerbread' figures cut out of spiced marzipan. If you prefer a thin layer of icing, halve the quantity.

MAKES 12–14

175g/6oz/¾ cup butter, softened
175g/6oz/¾ cup golden caster (superfine) sugar
3 eggs, lightly beaten
25ml/1½ tbsp black treacle (molasses)
35ml/2½ tbsp syrup from a jar of preserved ginger
225g/8oz/2 cups self-raising (self-rising) flour, sifted
10ml/2 tsp ground ginger
25ml/1½ tbsp ground almonds
30ml/2 tbsp single (light) cream

For the icing (halve the quantities if you want a thin layer of icing)
350g/12oz/3 cups icing (confectioners') sugar
60ml/4 tbsp lemon juice
10ml/2 tsp water

For the decoration
115g/4oz golden marzipan
2.5ml/½ tsp mixed (pumpkin pie) spice
a few drops ginger-brown food colouring

1 Preheat the oven to 180°C/350°F/Gas 4. Line the cups of a large bun tin (pan) with paper cases.

2 Beat the butter and sugar together until light and creamy. Gradually beat in the eggs in batches, beating well between each addition.

3 Fold in the black treacle and the ginger syrup.

4 Sift in the flour with the ground ginger and fold in lightly. Add the ground almonds, then the cream, and stir until well combined.

5 Half-fill the prepared cups and bake for 20 minutes, or until slightly springy to the touch. Leave for a few minutes. Turn out on to a wire rack.

6 To make the icing, sift the icing (confectioners') sugar into a bowl and gradually mix in the lemon juice until the mixture is smooth, adding the water if necessary to get the correct consistency.

7 When the cakes are completely cold, spoon the icing on to each one and smooth it level with a metal spatula.

8 To make the gingerbread figures, knead the ground spice and food colouring into the marzipan and roll it out thinly. Using a small gingerbread figure cutter, cut out the shapes and stick one to the top of each freshly iced cake.

Energy 314kcal/1320kJ; Protein 3.9g; Carbohydrate 45.6g, of which sugars 33.3g; Fat 14.1g, of which saturates 7.6g; Cholesterol 71mg; Calcium 64mg; Fibre 0.8g; Sodium 115mg.

Spangled sugar cupcakes

These cakes are made using a basic mixture, but are transformed by the original decoration using caramelized sugar spirals, which are not difficult to make. If you prefer, you can pour the caramel on to an oiled surface to set, then break it into transparent golden shards.

MAKES 8–9

175g/6oz/¾ cup butter, softened
175g/6oz/¾ cup caster (superfine) sugar
5ml/1 tsp vanilla extract or finely grated lemon rind
4 eggs, lightly beaten
175g/6oz/1½ cups self-raising (self-rising) flour, sifted
115g/4oz cinder toffee (honeycomb) broken into small pieces

For the pulled sugar decorations
115g/4oz/½ cup caster (superfine) sugar

1 Preheat the oven to 180°C/350°F/ Gas 4. Line the cups of a bun tin (pan) with paper cake cases.

2 Beat the softened butter with the sugar using an electric mixer until light and creamy. Add the vanilla extract or lemon rind. Gradually add the eggs in small amounts, beating well after each addition.

3 Add the sifted flour and fold it lightly into the mixture until just combined. Fold in the cinder toffee.

4 Spoon the mixture into the paper cases and bake for 20 minutes until the cakes are golden brown and feel firm to the touch.

5 Allow the cakes to cool a little in the tin, then turn them out on to a wire rack to cool completely.

6 To make the caramel, place the caster sugar in a non-stick pan over a medium to high heat. Do not stir. When the sugar starts to turn into syrup around the edges tilt the pan to blend the sugar into the syrup. Continue until all the sugar has melted into a golden caramel.

7 Remove the pan immediately from the heat and briefly sink its base in cold water. As the caramel cools it will become thicker; for sugar spirals it needs to be the consistency of golden (corn) syrup. If it thickens too much, gently warm it up.

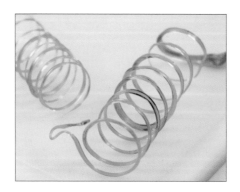

8 To make the spirals, take one tablespoonful of the caramel and trail it over a greased sharpening steel, while turning the steel. Snap off the tail of the caramel and gently slide the spiral off.

9 Leave on a lightly oiled tray while you make the remaining spiral decorations.

10 Gently press the sugar spirals at a 45-degree angle on top of the cakes. Sprinkle with a few crushed caramel threads to add a little sparkle, or some extra shards of cinder toffee, if you like. Serve with cream.

TO MAKE CINDER TOFFEE (HONEYCOMB)
Oil a baking tray. Place 400g/ 14oz/2 cups sugar, 100ml/3½fl oz/scant ½ cup clear honey and 30ml/2 tbsp liquid glucose in a heavy pan with 100ml/3½fl oz/ scant ½ cup water. Boil until a sugar thermometer reads 160°C/325°F, then remove from the heat. Instantly whisk in 7.5ml/1½ tsp bicarbonate of soda (baking soda) and quickly pour the mixture into the tray. It will bubble up, but will subside gradually. Leave to set.

Energy 569kcal/2379kJ; Protein 5.6g; Carbohydrate 61.6g, of which sugars 46.7g; Fat 37.7g, of which saturates 21.7g; Cholesterol 173mg; Calcium 81mg; Fibre 0.6g; Sodium 203mg.

Pear cakes with curled marzipan leaves

The glorious shapes and colours of fallen leaves inspired the decoration for these delicious cakes made with caramelized autumn fruit. If you prefer to make standard-sized cupcakes, cut the pears into chunks instead of halves.

3 Place the butter, sugar and water in a small frying pan over a low to medium heat, then sauté the pear halves gently for 6–7 minutes until tender. Set aside to cool.

4 Sift the dry ingredients into a large bowl. In another bowl, stir the egg, lemon rind, warm melted butter and sour cream together, then gently fold the mixture into the dry ingredients, with the pecans, until blended.

5 Add a small dollop of the batter to each cup. Press one pear half into each, standing it upright, then half-fill the tins with the remaining batter. (Half of the pear length and its stem should still be visible.)

6 Bake for 25 minutes. Leave to cool for 5 minutes, then turn out on to a wire rack. Serve dusted with icing sugar and decorated with curled marzipan leaves.

MAKES 6–7 LARGE CAKES

3–4 small ripe pears
40g/1½oz/3 tbsp butter
15ml/1 tbsp caster (superfine) sugar
45ml/3 tbsp water
225g/8oz/2 cups plain (all-purpose) flour
15ml/1 tbsp baking powder
10ml/2 tsp mixed (apple pie) spice
150g/5oz/¾ cup golden caster (superfine) sugar
1 egg, lightly beaten
5ml/1 tsp finely grated lemon rind
75g/3oz/6 tbsp butter, melted
300ml/½ pint/1¼ cups sour cream
20 pecan nuts, lightly crushed
marzipan leaves (see page 26) and sifted icing (confectioners') sugar, to decorate

1 Preheat the oven to 180°C/350°F/ Gas 4. Grease 6–7 10cm/4in-diameter muffin tins (pans) or line with mini panettone paper cases.

2 To prepare the fruit, peel and cut the pears into halves lengthways. Remove the cores but leave the short stems on the pieces of fruit wherever possible.

COOK'S TIP
Pan frying the pear halves in sugar and butter gives the fruit, and the muffins, more flavour.

Energy 566kcal/2362kJ; Protein 7.1g; Carbohydrate 58.7g, of which sugars 33.9g; Fat 35.2g, of which saturates 15.5g; Cholesterol 91mg; Calcium 121mg; Fibre 3.2g; Sodium 155mg.

Pistachio flower cupcakes

The pistachios add flavour and a delicate green colour to a basic friand cake mixture, which is lightly perfumed with rose water. These pretty flower-shaped cakes made in shallow fluted cake moulds will delight any lover of Parisian-style cakes.

MAKES 12

175g/6oz/¾ cup butter, melted
5ml/1 tsp rose water
150g/5oz/1¼ cups finely ground pistachios, sifted
225g/8oz/2 cups icing (confectioners') sugar, sifted, plus extra for dusting
70g/2½oz/9 tbsp plain (all-purpose) flour, sifted
6 egg whites
2.5ml/½ tsp finely grated lemon rind

1 Preheat the oven to 190°C/375°F/Gas 5. Grease 12 fluted bun tins (pans) or the cups of an oval friand tin with melted butter and dust lightly with flour. Tap the tray or fluted tins upside down on the work surface to get rid of the excess flour.

2 Mix the melted butter and rose water in a small bowl, then set aside.

3 Put the ground pistachios in a large mixing bowl, reserving 25g/1oz for decorating the cakes. Stir in the sifted icing sugar and flour.

4 In a separate bowl, beat the egg whites lightly just to break them up, about 15 seconds.

5 Add the egg whites to the dry ingredients and mix. Add the melted butter and lemon rind to the bowl and mix until just combined.

6 Pour the mixture into the prepared tins and bake for about 16 minutes or until pale golden around the edges and springy to the touch. Leave to cool slightly then turn out on to a wire rack.

7 Dust the cakes with the reserved pistachios. Half-cover them with a strip of paper and dust with icing sugar, then carefully remove the paper.

Energy 282kcal/1177kJ; Protein 4.4g; Carbohydrate 25.2g, of which sugars 20.4g; Fat 18.9g, of which saturates 8.8g; Cholesterol 34mg; Calcium 35mg; Fibre 0.9g; Sodium 207mg.

Chocolate and vanilla cupcakes

A snowy topping of thick, creamy mascarpone whipped with sugar and flecked with the fragrant black seeds of vanilla conceals a lovely dark cake: the intense and slightly bitter chocolate flavour contrasts perfectly with the smooth, sweet icing.

MAKES 10

50g/2oz dark (bittersweet) chocolate, melted
115g/4oz/½ cup butter, melted
100g/3½oz/scant ½ cup caster (superfine) sugar
115g/4oz/1 cup self-raising (self-rising) flour, sifted
3 eggs, lightly beaten
50g/2oz/½ cup ground almonds
5ml/1 tsp vanilla extract

For the topping
175g/6oz/¾ cup butter, softened
2.5ml/½ tsp finely grated lemon rind
350g/12oz/3 cups icing (confectioner's) sugar, sifted, plus extra for dusting
225g/8oz/1 cup mascarpone
10ml/2 tsp double-strength espresso coffee (optional)
½ vanilla pod (bean)

1 Preheat the oven to 180°C/350°F/Gas 4. Line a muffin tin (pan) with paper cases.

2 Scrape the seeds from the vanilla pod and reserve. Cut the pod into fine, short strips.

3 Mix the sugar with the flour. Stir in the eggs and add the melted butter, ground almonds and vanilla extract, followed by the melted chocolate. Stir together, then cover the bowl and chill for 30 minutes to 1 hour.

4 Spoon the mixture into the muffin cases, filling three-quarters full.

5 Bake for 25 minutes, or until the cakes are firm. Leave to cool.

6 For the topping, in a bowl beat the butter, lemon rind, sugar and mascarpone until smooth. Stir in the coffee, if using, and vanilla seeds. Pipe on the cakes. Dust with icing sugar and top with the vanilla strips.

Energy 608kcal/2537kJ; Protein 5.3g; Carbohydrate 59.6g, of which sugars 50.4g; Fat 40.4g, of which saturates 23.9g; Cholesterol 146mg; Calcium 89mg; Fibre 0.7g; Sodium 310mg.

Montebianco cupcakes

This recipe is based on a pudding called Marrons Mont Blanc in France and Montebianco in Italy. A sweetened chestnut purée is covered in thick vanilla cream: anyone with a sweet tooth and a passion for chestnuts will find these little cakes especially delicious.

MAKES 10

75g/3oz/6 tbsp butter, softened
175g/6oz/¾ cup golden caster (superfine) sugar
115g/4oz/1 cup icing (confectioners') sugar
5ml/1 tsp vanilla extract
15ml/1 tbsp rum
4 eggs, separated
200g/7oz cooked and peeled whole chestnuts, ground
150g/5oz/1¼ cups plain (all-purpose) flour
10ml/2 tsp baking powder

For the topping
300ml/½ pint/1¼ cups double (heavy) cream
5ml/1 tsp vanilla extract
10ml/2 tsp caster (superfine) sugar
sifted cocoa powder, to dust

1 Preheat the oven to 180°C/350°F/ Gas 4. Line the cups of a bun tin (pan) with paper cases.

2 Place the butter, caster sugar and icing sugar in a large bowl and beat until light and smooth using an electric mixer. Mix in the vanilla extract and rum.

3 Beat the egg yolks lightly and add them in a thin stream, beating well until the mixture is very smooth. Add the ground chestnuts and beat them in, then fold in the flour sifted together with the baking powder.

4 In a separate bowl beat the egg whites into fairly firm peaks and fold them lightly into the chestnut mixture until evenly combined.

5 Fill the cups three-quarters full with the cake mixture, and bake for 20–25 minutes, until the cakes are golden and the centres feel springy. Remove from the oven.

6 Leave the cakes in the tins for 5 minutes to cool, then turn them out on to a wire rack and leave them to cool completely.

7 To make the topping, beat the cream with the vanilla extract and caster sugar into soft peaks that hold their shape. Transfer to a large piping (pastry) bag fitted with a plain 5mm/¼in nozzle and pipe into tall piles.

8 To finish, dust the cream very lightly with sifted cocoa powder.

Energy 429kcal/1796kJ; Protein 5g; Carbohydrate 51.1g, of which sugars 33.8g; Fat 25.2g, of which saturates 13.8g; Cholesterol 132mg; Calcium 74mg; Fibre 1.3g; Sodium 100mg.

Carrot cupcakes

These wonderfully tasty cakes are made using an easy all-in-one recipe. The mixture is enriched with grated carrots, which add sweetness as well as keeping the cakes moist and light. The chopped nuts impart extra flavour and texture. Little marzipan carrots are the classic decoration.

MAKES 8–10

225g/8oz/1 cup caster
   (superfine) sugar
3 eggs
200ml/7fl oz/scant 1 cup
   vegetable oil
grated rind and juice of 1 orange
225g/8oz/2 cups self-raising
   (self-rising) wholemeal
   (whole-wheat) flour
5ml/1 tsp ground cinnamon
2.5ml/½ tsp grated nutmeg
pinch of salt
350g/12oz grated carrot,
   squeezed dry
175g/6oz/1 cup walnuts, chopped

For the topping
225g/8oz/1 cup cream cheese
30ml/2 tbsp clear honey
15ml/1 tbsp orange juice
20 marzipan carrots

1 Preheat the oven to 180°C/350°F/ Gas 4. Line a bun tin (pan) with paper cases.

2 Beat the sugar, eggs, oil, orange rind and juice together until light and frothy. Sift in the flour, spices and salt and beat for a further minute. Stir in the carrots and nuts.

3 Fill the prepared paper cases and bake for 20–25 minutes, until the cakes are firm in the centre. Turn out on to a wire rack to cool.

4 To make the icing, beat the cheese, honey and orange juice together until smooth. Chill for 30 minutes.

5 Tint the marzipan with the food colouring to resemble the colour of carrots. Break off small pieces and roll between your palms to form carrot shapes.

6 Using a small knife, press marks around the carrots and stick small pieces of angelica in the top of each one to resemble stalks.

7 Remove the icing from the refrigerator and spread over the tops of the cooled cakes. Arrange the carrots on the cakes.

Energy 542kcal/2258kJ; Protein 7.9g; Carbohydrate 46.9g, of which sugars 32.7g; Fat 37.1g, of which saturates 9.6g; Cholesterol 78mg; Calcium 75mg; Fibre 3.4g; Sodium 102mg.

Dark chocolate cupcakes

Ground almonds replace most of the flour in these chocolatey sponge cakes, giving a very rich, deliciously moist result that needs very little adornment: instead of icing, the cakes have been simply finished with a generous dusting of sugar.

MAKES 12

175g/6oz/¾ cup butter
50g/2oz plain (semisweet) chocolate, broken up
7.5ml/1½ tsp finely grated orange rind
115g/4oz/1 cup ground almonds
115g/4oz/1 cup icing (confectioners') sugar, sifted
70g/2½oz/9 tbsp plain (all-purpose) flour, sifted
15ml/1 tbsp unsweetened cocoa powder
6 egg whites

1 Preheat the oven to 190°C/375°F/ Gas 5. Grease the cups of a bun tin (pan). Melt the butter with the chocolate and add the orange rind. Set aside to cool slightly.

2 Put the almonds in a large bowl and sift in the icing sugar, flour and cocoa powder.

3 In a separate bowl, beat the egg whites lightly for 15 seconds, just to break them up. Add the egg white to the dry ingredients and mix. Add the melted mixture to the bowl and mix until just combined.

4 Pour the mixture into the bun tin and bake for about 18 minutes, until the cakes are springy to the touch. Leave to cool slightly then turn out on to a wire rack.

5 Dust the cakes with icing sugar to serve, laying a card heart template over each one. Remove it carefully.

VARIATION
Decorate the cakes with chocolate hearts. Spread melted chocolate on to a cool surface. Leave until just set, then cut out the shapes. Dust with cocoa and chill. Attach a single heart to the top of each cake with a little sieved jam or icing.

Energy 255kcal/1063kJ; Protein 4.6g; Carbohydrate 18.1g, of which sugars 13g; Fat 18.8g, of which saturates 9.2g; Cholesterol 34mg; Calcium 42mg; Fibre 1g; Sodium 154mg.

Fish cakes

Multicoloured sugarpaste shapes make effective decorations with minimal effort. This technique makes good use of leftover scraps of different coloured sugarpastes, but the paste dries and hardens very quickly, so keep it well wrapped when you are not working with it.

MAKES 12

225g/8oz/1 cup butter, softened
225g/8oz/1 cup caster (superfine) sugar
4 eggs
225g/8oz/2 cups self-raising (self-rising) flour
115g/4oz/1 cup plain (all-purpose) flour
60ml/4 tbsp ground almonds
25ml/1½ tbsp lemon juice
15ml/1 tbsp milk

For the marbled toppings
275g/10oz sugarpaste
paste food colouring in 5 colours
a little blue royal icing

For the fish decorations
150g/5oz sugarpaste
paste food colouring in 6 colours
1 egg white, lightly beaten

1 Preheat the oven to 180°C/350°F/ Gas 4. Line a 12-cup bun tin (pan) with paper cases.

2 Beat the butter and sugar together until light and fluffy. Add two of the eggs, a little at a time, beating well after each addition.

3 Beat in 15ml/1 tbsp of the flour. Gradually add the remaining eggs, then beat in another 15ml/ 1 tbsp flour.

4 Sift the remaining flours and fold them in lightly with the almonds, lemon juice and milk.

5 Fill the paper cases almost to the top. Bake for 20–25 minutes, until the cakes are a light golden colour and the tops spring back when pressed. Transfer to a wire rack to go cold. Slice the top off each cake to level the surface.

6 To make the marbled toppings, divide the sugarpaste into five pieces and tint each piece a different colour. Divide each of the coloured pieces into 12 small balls.

7 Dust the work surface with icing (confectioners') sugar. Press a ball of each colour together in a circle. Roll out and cut out a circle to fit the top of a cupcake using a scallop-edged cutter. Cut one for each cake.

8 To make the stripy fish, divide the sugarpaste into six pieces and tint each with a different food colour. Roll each piece into a sausage, 10cm/4in long and 1cm/½in thick. Paint each strip with egg white and sandwich them together. Cut 12 slices from the slab.

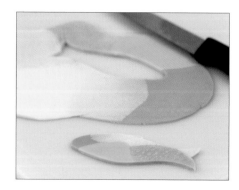

9 Roll out one slice to make a piece large enough for the fish shape. Cut out the fish and make 11 more. Spread a little royal icing on top of each cake. Press on a marbled circle and stick a fish on top.

Energy 504kcal/2121kJ; Protein 6.2g; Carbohydrate 79g, of which sugars 57.3g; Fat 20.4g, of which saturates 10.9g; Cholesterol 107mg; Calcium 94mg; Fibre 1.3g; Sodium 169mg.

Special occasion cakes

Prettily decorated cupcakes always look lovely on a party table. A tiered cakestand holding small cakes is a charming and popular substitute for a traditional wedding cake, but there is a design here for every occasion, from iced cakes encrusted with brightly coloured candies for a children's birthday tea to sophisticated liqueur-laced creations for grown-up feasts. Everyone enjoys helping themselves to their own beautifully iced little cake.

Christening cupcakes

Everyone will love these delicate little cakes, which are perfect for a christening party. Adorn the tops with cute decorations – rabbits, rocking horses and tiny spring flowers. For a small party halve the ingredients to make 24 bitesize cupcakes.

3 Add the sifted flour and fold it into the mixture using a metal spoon, until just combined.

4 Half-fill the paper cases with the cake mixture. Bake for 12–15 minutes until golden. Test by lightly pressing the centre of the cakes with your finger: the sponge should lightly spring back. Leave on a wire rack to cool.

5 To make the icing, sift the sugar into a mixing bowl and stir in the clementine juice until the consistency is smooth and shiny. Spread a little icing over the top of each cake, coaxing it lightly with a knife to coat the surface evenly.

6 Cut out sugarpaste decorations and arrange before the icing sets.

MAKES 48 TINY CAKES

175g/6oz/³⁄₄ cup butter, softened
175g/6oz/³⁄₄ cup caster (superfine) sugar
4 eggs, lightly beaten
5ml/1 tsp vanilla extract
175g/6oz/1½ cups self-raising (self-rising) flour, sifted

For the clementine icing
150g/5oz/1¼ cups icing (confectioners') sugar, sifted
freshly squeezed juice of 1 clementine or mandarin

For the decorations
115g/4oz sugarpaste divided and half tinted pink and half blue

1 Preheat the oven to 180°C/350°F/ Gas 4. Line the cups of four 12-cup mini cupcake trays with paper cases.

2 Place the softened butter and sugar in the bowl of an electric mixer and beat until light and creamy. Gradually add the beaten eggs in small amounts and beat well after each addition. Stir in the vanilla extract.

Energy 78kcal/329kJ; Protein 0.9g; Carbohydrate 11.6g, of which sugars 8.9g; Fat 3.5g, of which saturates 2.1g; Cholesterol 24mg; Calcium 20mg; Fibre 0.1g; Sodium 47mg.

Mini party cakes

These little cakes look extremely pretty decorated with icing and sugarpaste ornaments in different pastel colours. Once the cakes are iced a sherbet 'flying saucer' sweet is stuck on top of each one, before being decorated with butterflies and flowers.

MAKES 48 TINY CAKES

175g/6oz/¾ cup butter, softened
175g/6oz/¾ cup caster (superfine)
  sugar
4 eggs, lightly beaten
5ml/1 tsp vanilla extract
175g/6oz/1½ cups self-raising
  (self-rising) flour, sifted

For the icing
150g/5oz/1¼ cups icing
  (confectioners') sugar, sifted
food colouring in 4 colours: pink,
  pale blue, peach, green

For the decorations
115g/4oz white sugarpaste
food colouring in 4 colours: pink,
  pale blue, peach, green
sherbet-filled flying saucer sweets

1 Preheat the oven to 180°C/350°F/
Gas 4. Line the cups of four 12-cup
mini cupcake trays with paper cases.

2 Place the softened butter and
sugar in the bowl of an electric
mixer and beat until light and
creamy. Gradually add the eggs in
small amounts and beat well after
each addition.

3 Add the vanilla and sifted flour
and fold it into the butter mixture
until just combined.

4 Half-fill the paper cases with
the mixture and bake for 12–15
minutes until golden. Test by
pressing the centre of the cakes with
your finger: the sponge should
lightly spring back. Leave on a wire
rack to cool completely.

5 Make the icing with just enough
hot water (about 20ml/4 tsp) to
make a soft glacé icing. Divide the
icing between four bowls, then tint
each with a different food colour,
keeping the colours pale.

6 Ice each cake and coax it to the
edges with the back of the spoon.

7 Decorate flying saucer sweets
with tinted sprinkles and sugarpaste
flowers, leaves and butterflies. Attach
with glacé icing. Stick each to the
top of a cupcake with glacé icing.

Energy 78kcal/329kJ; Protein 0.9g; Carbohydrate 11.6g, of which sugars 8.9g; Fat 3.5g, of which saturates 2.1g; Cholesterol 24mg; Calcium 20mg; Fibre 0.1g; Sodium 47mg.

Lovebirds

Unashamedly romantic decorations make these cakes perfect for any occasion when love is in the air, from an intimate tryst to an engagement or anniversary party. They would also make a sweet gift for a loving couple, nestled in a pretty box.

MAKES 10

175g/6oz/¾ cup butter, softened
175g/6oz/¾ cup caster (superfine) sugar
4 eggs, lightly beaten
5ml/1 tsp vanilla extract
175g/6oz/1½ cups self-raising (self-rising) flour, sifted

For the icing and decorations
350g/12oz/3 cups icing (confectioners') sugar, sifted
115g/4oz white sugarpaste
food colour in different tints

1 Preheat the oven to 180°C/350°F/ Gas 4. Line a bun tin (pan) with paper cases.

2 Beat the butter with the sugar until creamy.

3 Beat in the eggs one at a time, then stir in the vanilla and flour.

4 Half-fill the paper cases with the batter. Bake for 20 minutes, until golden. Cool on a wire rack.

5 Tint the sugarpaste and cut out scalloped circles to fit the cake tops.

6 Make the glacé icing, then tint it and spread a little on each cake. Stick one scallop to each cake top.

7 Cut out lovebirds, hearts, flowers, and leaves. Leave to dry flat.

8 Stick the decorations in place as desired with sugarpaste and icing.

Energy 385kcal/1614kJ; Protein 4.9g; Carbohydrate 52.8g, of which sugars 38g; Fat 18.6g, of which saturates 11.2g; Cholesterol 129mg; Calcium 62mg; Fibre 0.6g; Sodium 180mg.

Valentine cupcakes

Pink and white sugared hearts make a classic cake decoration that's very easy to achieve, using a few cutters in different sizes. Just mix and match the colours and designs on a batch of cakes to give a contemporary twist to this traditional theme for Valentine's Day.

MAKES 10

175g/6oz/³⁄₄ cup butter, softened
175g/6oz/³⁄₄ cup caster (superfine) sugar
4 eggs, lightly beaten
5ml/1 tsp vanilla extract
175g/6oz/1½ cups self-raising (self-rising) flour, sifted

For the topping
350g/12oz icing (confectioners') sugar, sifted
115g/4oz white sugarpaste
pink food colouring
pink candy sugar or sprinkles

1 Preheat the oven to 180°C/350°F/ Gas 4. Line the cups of a bun tin (pan) with paper cases.

2 Beat the butter and sugar until light and creamy. Gradually add the beaten eggs in small amounts and beat well after each addition. Stir in the vanilla extract. Add the sifted flour and fold it into the mixture until just combined.

3 Spoon the mixture into the paper cases. Bake in the centre of the oven for 20 minutes until golden. Test by lightly pressing the centre of the cakes with your finger: the sponge should lightly spring back. Leave on a wire rack to cool completely.

4 To make the topping, mix the sugar with enough hot water to make a fairly thick icing. Divide between two bowls and tint one pink. Spread on to the cakes.

5 Cut out heart shapes using different size cutters and different shades of pink sugarpaste. Place on a flat surface to dry.

6 Stick the decorations on the iced cakes. Paint some of the hearts with water and cover with pink candy sugar or sprinkles before attaching.

Energy 501kcal/2109kJ; Protein 5g; Carbohydrate 83.6g, of which sugars 68.8g; Fat 18.6g, of which saturates 11.2g; Cholesterol 129mg; Calcium 78mg; Fibre 0.6g; Sodium 181mg.

Marzipan-topped Easter cakes

These Easter cupcakes are irresistibly flavoured with fresh spices and orange zest and decorated with an embossed marzipan topping and cute little Easter motifs. If you are making the cakes for children, you could soak the dried fruit in orange juice instead of sherry.

MAKES 10–11

115g/4oz dried mango or pineapple or a mixture, finely chopped
115g/4oz sultanas (golden raisins)
50g/2oz mixed (candied) peel, chopped
100ml/3½ fl oz/scant ½ cup sherry
115g/4oz/½ cup butter, softened
115g/4oz/½ cup light muscovado (brown) sugar
2 eggs
225g/8oz/2 cups self-raising (self-rising) flour
7.5ml/1½ tsp mixed (apple pie) spice
finely grated rind of ½ large orange and juice of ¼ orange

For the apricot glaze
30ml/2 tbsp apricot jam
15ml/1 tbsp water
15ml/1 tbsp caster (superfine) sugar

For the topping
450g/1lb marzipan
small amounts of sugarpaste in white, primrose yellow, pale blue and pale pink
a little royal icing
sugared eggs

1 Place the dried fruits in a bowl with the mixed (candied) peel. Add the sherry and stir well. Leave for 24 hours.

2 Preheat the oven to 180°C/350°F/Gas 4. Line the cups of a bun tin (pan) with paper cases.

3 Beat the butter and sugar until creamy. Beat in an egg. Add 15ml/1 tbsp of flour and mix well before repeating with the second egg and another 15ml/1 tbsp flour. Fold in the remaining flour and mixed spice. Drain the dried fruit and stir it in with the orange rind and juice.

4 Fill the paper cases three-quarters full. Bake for 22–25 minutes until springy to the touch. Allow to cool completely. Slice off the tops level with the top of the cases.

5 Put the apricot glaze ingredients in a pan and melt over a low heat.

6 Roll out the marzipan to 3mm/⅛in thick. Emboss with circular patterns. Cut out using a round cutter and attach to the cakes using the glaze.

7 Cut out and decorate a selection of motifs from sugarpaste and leave on a flat surface to dry before sticking in place with a little royal icing, along with a few sugared eggs.

Energy 452kcal/1903kJ; Protein 5.8g; Carbohydrate 73.7g, of which sugars 58.1g; Fat 15.1g, of which saturates 6.5g; Cholesterol 59mg; Calcium 85mg; Fibre 2g; Sodium 127mg.

You're a star!

Mascarpone and Marsala add a delicious nuance to these mocha-flavoured cakes, which are topped with a smooth velvety cream and decorated with chocolate stars. You can make the chocolate decorations in advance and keep them in an airtight box in the refrigerator.

MAKES 8–10

150g/5oz/10 tbsp butter, softened
200g/7oz/scant 1 cup golden caster (superfine) sugar
3 eggs
175g/6oz/¾ cup mascarpone
5ml/1 tsp grated lemon rind
30ml/2 tbsp buttermilk
15ml/1 tbsp unsweetened cocoa powder, plus extra for dusting
25ml/1½ tbsp espresso coffee
15ml/1 tbsp Marsala
250g/9oz/2¼ cups self-raising (self-rising) flour

For the topping
250ml/8fl oz/1 cup double (heavy) cream
225g/8oz/1 cup mascarpone
15ml/1 tbsp golden caster (superfine) sugar
15ml/1 tbsp Marsala
seeds from ½ vanilla pod (bean)
25g/1oz milk chocolate, melted

For the chocolate stars and leaves
100g/3½oz plain (semisweet) chocolate
100g/3½oz milk chocolate

1 Preheat the oven to 180°C/350°F/ Gas 4. Line a muffin tin (pan) with paper cases.

2 Beat the butter and sugar together until light and creamy. Gradually beat in the eggs, one at a time, beating well after each addition. Stir in the mascarpone, lemon rind, buttermilk, cocoa, coffee and Marsala, then fold in the flour.

3 Fill the prepared cups. Bake for 25 minutes, or until firm to the touch. Turn out on to a wire rack to cool.

4 Meanwhile, make the topping. Beat the cream with the mascarpone, sugar, Marsala and vanilla seeds. Lightly fold in the melted chocolate.

5 To make the decorations, melt the chocolates separately, then spread on baking parchment and chill until just set. Cut out the shapes.

6 Spoon the topping on to the cakes, and press on the decorations. Dust with cocoa powder.

Energy 718kcal/2990kJ; Protein 8g; Carbohydrate 56.8g, of which sugars 36.7g; Fat 53.7g, of which saturates 32.1g; Cholesterol 167mg; Calcium 146mg; Fibre 1g; Sodium 297mg.

Mother's Day fairy cakes with sugar roses

These deliciously featherlight sponge cakes are topped with delicately coloured icing scented with rose water and trimmed with a feminine melange of sugarpaste flower decorations. Silver foil cases will add a touch of glamour to these very special cakes.

MAKES 10

3 eggs, separated
115g/4oz/½ cup caster (superfine) sugar
juice of ½ lemon
grated rind of 1 mandarin
65g/2½oz/scant ½ cup fine semolina
15g/½oz/1 tbsp ground almonds

For the rose water icing
350g/12oz/3 cups icing (confectioners') sugar
5ml/1 tsp rose water
15ml/1 tbsp hot water

For the decorations
350g/12oz white sugarpaste
food colouring

1 Preheat the oven to 180°C/350°F/ Gas 4. Line the cups of a bun tin (pan) with foil or paper cases.

2 Beat the egg yolks with the sugar until light. Beat in the lemon juice and fold in the mandarin rind, semolina and almonds. In a separate bowl, whisk the egg whites until stiff. Fold into the mixture.

3 Pour into the cake cases until half full. Bake for 15 minutes, until the cakes are golden. Leave to cool, then turn out on to a wire rack.

4 To make the icing, mix the sugar with the rose water and enough hot water to make a flowing consistency. Spread it on top of the cooled cakes and leave to dry.

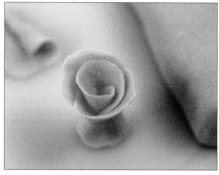

5 To make the sugarpaste roses, tint some paste pink and roll out 3–4 small circles very thinly; roll up the first to form the centre then add the other petals working around the central petal. Keep the petals open at the top so that they start to resemble an unfurling bud. Set all the flowers on a board covered with baking parchment to dry. Stick in place with a small blob of icing.

Energy 306kcal/1302kJ; Protein 3.2g; Carbohydrate 72g, of which sugars 66.9g; Fat 2.6g, of which saturates 0.5g; Cholesterol 57mg; Calcium 47mg; Fibre 0.3g; Sodium 26mg.

Summer cupcakes with fresh fruit icing

Add a touch of indulgence to a summer tea party with these gloriously pretty cupcakes. The recipe is simple and the cakes are topped with a trio of icings flavoured with fresh fruit juice, then decorated with sugarpaste flowers easily created using plunger cutters.

MAKES 12

225g/8oz/1 cup butter, softened
225g/8oz/1 cup caster (superfine)
   sugar
4 eggs, lightly beaten
50g/2oz/½ cup plain (all-purpose)
   flour
150g/5oz/1¼ cups ground almonds
5ml/1 tsp vanilla extract
15ml/1 tbsp single (light) cream

For the decorations
350g/12oz white sugarpaste
food colouring
royal icing
artificial flower stamens
candy sugar, for sprinkling

For the icing
350g/12oz/3 cups icing
   (confectioners') sugar, sifted
15ml/1 tbsp fresh raspberry juice
15ml/1 tbsp fresh orange juice
15ml/1 tbsp fresh lime juice

1 Preheat the oven to 180°C/350°F/ Gas 4. Line the cups of a bun tin (pan) with paper cases.

2 Beat the butter and sugar until light and creamy. Add the eggs in small amounts, beating well after each addition. Sift in the flour and beat well. Add the ground almonds, vanilla extract and cream and combine.

3 Part fill the paper cases and bake for 20–25 minutes until the cakes are light golden brown and the centres feel firm to the touch.

4 Leave the cakes to cool in the tin for 5 minutes, then turn out on to a wire rack to cool completely.

5 To make the flowers, tint pieces of paste as desired. Roll out and stamp out individual petals. Stick together arranging them in a flower shape.

6 Mount some stamens in royal icing. Leave to dry. Cut out small flowers using plunger cutters.

7 When the decorations are dry, make the icing for the cake tops. Divide the sugar among three bowls and mix each batch with one of the fruit juices and about 5ml/1 tsp hot water to make a smooth fluid icing.

8 Spread each icing on top of the cakes, coaxing it out to the edges. Arrange the sugarpaste decorations on the cakes before the icing sets.

9 Once it is dry, sprinkle some of the cakes with a little candy sugar.

Energy 536kcal/2253kJ; Protein 5.6g; Carbohydrate 78.4g, of which sugars 74.9g; Fat 24.4g, of which saturates 11.4g; Cholesterol 107mg; Calcium 87mg; Fibre 1.1g; Sodium 171mg.

Iced cherry cakes

Glacé cherries are used in this almond cake mixture, but if you find them too sweet you could use sharp-tasting dried sour cherries, or even fresh cherries. You'll need a special textured rolling pin to achieve the lovely embossed basketweave design on the icing.

3 In another bowl beat the butter and sugar until creamy. Add one egg at a time and beat until the mixture is light and fluffy. Mix in the fruit rind, brandy and orange juice, then the dry ingredients and the cherries.

4 Fill the paper cases three-quarters full. Bake for 25 minutes or until golden and springy to the touch. Leave to cool a little before turning them out on to a wire rack.

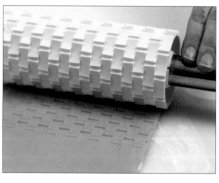

MAKES 10

175g/6oz/1½ cups self-raising (self-rising) flour
10ml/2 tsp baking powder
75g/3oz/¾ cup ground almonds
175g/6oz/¾ cup butter, softened
175g/6oz/¾ cup golden caster (superfine) sugar
3 eggs, lightly beaten
finely grated rind of ½ lemon
finely grated rind of ½ orange
15ml/1 tbsp brandy or Calvados
60ml/4 tbsp orange juice
150g/5oz glacé cherries, halved

For the topping
350g/12oz sugarpaste
green food colouring

For the decorations
150g/5oz sugarpaste
red and brown food colouring
115g/4oz royal icing

1 Preheat the oven to 180°C/350°F/ Gas 4. Line the cups of a bun tin (pan) with paper cases.

2 Sift the flour and baking powder into a mixing bowl and stir in the ground almonds.

5 For the topping, colour the sugarpaste pale green and roll it out to a 6mm/¼in thickness. Emboss with a decorative rolling pin then cut out 10 circles and stick them on the cooled cakes using royal icing. Roll 20 red sugarpaste cherries, 20 brown stems and some green leaves and stick in place.

Energy 548kcal/2308kJ; Protein 5.6g; Carbohydrate 90.4g, of which sugars 76.9g; Fat 20.4g, of which saturates 10.3g; Cholesterol 97mg; Calcium 96mg; Fibre 1.2g; Sodium 162mg.

Wedding cupcakes

The pink or peach sugarpaste circular toppings will stand slightly proud of the cakes, so make them a little in advance so that they firm up before they are applied, with royal icing, to the tops of the cakes. Use ready-made sugar flowers or make your own using a plunger cutter.

MAKES 12

225g/8oz marzipan
75g/3oz/6 tbsp butter, softened
100g/3½oz/scant ½ cup caster (superfine) sugar
3 eggs, lightly beaten
15ml/1 tbsp brandy
100g/3½oz/scant ½ cup ground almonds
150g/5oz/1¼ cups plain (all-purpose) flour
10ml/2 tsp baking powder

For the topping
450g/1lb white sugarpaste
paste food colouring in pink or peach and apple green
115g/4oz royal icing
sugarpaste flowers

1 To make the sugarpaste circles colour 175g/6oz of the sugarpaste shell pink or peach. Roll it out fairly thinly on a surface dusted with icing (confectioners') sugar. Using a round crinkle-edged cutter stamp out 12 circles and leave them to dry.

2 To make the scalloped circles roll out 140–175g/5–6oz of white sugarpaste fairly thinly. Stamp out 12 circles a little smaller than the pink circles. Leave to dry.

3 To make the leaves, colour the remaining 115g/4oz of sugarpaste apple green (or leave it white if you like). Roll it out thinly and using a leaf cutter stamp out 12 leaves. Lightly bend them into realistic shapes and leave to dry.

4 Preheat the oven to 180°C/350°F/ Gas 4. Line the cups of a muffin tin (pan) with paper cases.

5 Place the marzipan, butter and sugar together in the bowl of an electric mixer and mix well to a smooth even paste. Leaving the motor running, add the eggs in a very thin stream, beating well until the mixture is smooth.

6 Add the brandy and ground almonds, sift in the flour and baking powder and fold in.

7 Fill the cups three-quarters full with the cake mixture, and bake for 20–25 minutes until the cakes are golden and the centres are springy to the touch.

8 Leave to cool in the tin for 5 minutes, then turn the cakes out on to a wire rack and leave to cool completely.

9 Use a blob of royal icing to attach the scalloped circles to the cake toppings. Brush the cakes with a little more icing and press the circles on top, then decorate with sugarpaste leaves and flowers.

Energy 302kcal/1269kJ; Protein 5.6g; Carbohydrate 40.4g, of which sugars 30.6g; Fat 13.7g, of which saturates 4.4g; Cholesterol 62mg; Calcium 67mg; Fibre 1.4g; Sodium 71mg.

Welcome to your new home cupcakes

The hand-piped decorations on these cakes may look ambitious but with care you can achieve the pattern quite easily. You will need several small piping bags with fine plain nozzles filled with different coloured royal icing to infill the details of the houses and flower borders.

MAKES 12

2 eggs
115g/4oz/½ cup caster
   (superfine) sugar
50ml/2fl oz/¼ cup double
   (heavy) cream
finely grated rind of 1 small lemon
finely grated rind of 1 small orange
115g/4oz/1 cup self-raising (self-
   rising) flour
2.5ml/½ tsp baking powder
50g/2oz/4 tbsp butter, melted

For the icing

350g/12oz/3 cups icing
   (confectioners') sugar, sifted
15ml/1 tbsp clementine or orange
   juice, strained

For the decoration

sugarpaste coloured as desired
225g/8oz royal icing
food colouring in several shades

1 Preheat the oven to 180°C/350°F/Gas 4. Line the cups of a 12-hole bun tin (pan) with paper cases.

2 Beat the eggs with the sugar until pale in colour. Beat in the cream, then add the grated lemon and orange rinds. Fold in the flour sifted with the baking powder, then fold in the warm melted butter.

3 Three-quarters fill the cases and bake for about 15 minutes, until golden. Leave to cool completely.

4 Roll out the sugarpaste on a light dusting of icing sugar and cut scallop edge circles to fit each cake.

5 Mix the icing sugar with enough fruit juice to make a thick, fluid consistency. Spread over the cakes and immediately stick a sugarpaste scallop to each.

6 To make the houses, tint the royal icing as desired to a soft consistency and fill several piping bags fitted with fine plain nozzles.

7 On to the sugarpaste scallop, pipe a square for the house shape. Fill with icing and smooth out any air bubbles. Add a roof and then a chimney in the same way

8 Pipe all the decorative details.

Energy 305kcal/1290kJ; Protein 2.3g; Carbohydrate 63.3g, of which sugars 56g; Fat 6.7g, of which saturates 3.8g; Cholesterol 47mg; Calcium 49mg; Fibre 0.3g; Sodium 48mg.

Party number cakes

These delicious, moist Madeira cakes have a hidden centre of tangy lemon curd. The pretty pastel-coloured alphabet candies that decorate them can be arranged to spell out the names of your guests, if you wish. Look out for delicately coloured sweets and sprinkles to complete the effect.

MAKES 12

225g/8oz/1 cup butter, softened
225g/8oz/1 cup caster (superfine)
  sugar
4 eggs
225g/8oz/2 cups self-raising
  (self-rising) flour
115g/4oz/1 cup plain (all-purpose)
  flour
60ml/4 tbsp ground almonds
25ml/1½ tbsp lemon juice
15ml/1 tbsp milk
60ml/4 tbsp lemon curd

For the sherbet icing
250g/9oz/2¼ cups icing
  (confectioners') sugar,
  double sifted
40g/1½oz/⅓ cup sherbet
30ml/2 tbsp lemon juice
20ml/4 tsp hot water
15ml/1 tbsp lemon curd

For the decorations
60 alphabet sweets (candies)
36 torpedo sweets (candies)
candy sugar or sprinkles

1 Preheat the oven to 180°C/350°F/ Gas 4. Line the cups of a 12-cup muffin tin (pan) with paper cases.

2 Cream the butter and sugar until light and fluffy. Beat in two eggs a little at a time, then 15ml/1 tbsp of the flour. Add the remaining eggs, and another 15ml/1 tbsp of flour.

3 Sift the remaining flours in, then fold them in lightly with the ground almonds, lemon juice and milk.

4 Fill the paper cups almost to the top. Bake for 20–25 minutes until the cakes are golden. Allow to cool.

5 To make the sherbet icing, sift the sugar and sherbet and combine with the remaining ingredients to make a soft icing that is just firm enough to hold its shape.

6 When the cakes are cold, slice a round from the top of each one. Insert 5ml/1 tsp lemon curd into each cake before replacing the top.

7 Spread each cake with a thick layer of sherbet icing. Press your choice of decorations into the icing while it is soft.

Energy 464kcal/1950kJ; Protein 6.2g; Carbohydrate 67.7g, of which sugars 44.6g; Fat 20.7g, of which saturates 11g; Cholesterol 108mg; Calcium 87mg; Fibre 1.3g; Sodium 173mg.

Wedding anniversary cakes

Delicious featherlight cakes and simple white and mauve sugarpaste hearts make an elegant presentation for an anniversary celebration. The decorations are easy to make with a heart-shaped cutter and a tiny flower-shaped plunger cutter.

MAKES 10

3 eggs, separated
115g/4oz/½ cup caster (superfine) sugar
juice of ½ lemon
grated rind of 1 mandarin
65g/2½oz/scant ½ cup fine semolina
15g/½oz/1 tbsp ground almonds

For the icing
350g/12oz/3 cups icing (confectioners') sugar
5ml/1 tsp grappa
15ml/1 tbsp hot water

For the decorations
350g/12oz white sugarpaste
mauve food colouring
a little royal icing

1 To make the decorations, divide the sugarpaste in half. Knead a little mauve food colouring into one piece until evenly coloured, then roll out both pieces separately. Cut out 10 mauve hearts and 10 white hearts.

2 Cut out 20 small flowers and pipe a little royal icing into each centre. Leave the decorations to dry.

3 Preheat the oven to 180°C/350°F/ Gas 4. Line the cups of a bun tin (pan) with paper cases.

4 Using an electric mixer, beat the egg yolks with the sugar until light and creamy. Add the lemon juice and beat until well mixed. Fold in the grated mandarin rind, semolina and ground almonds using a large spoon or spatula.

5 In a separate bowl, whisk the egg whites until stiff peaks form.

6 Lightly stir one heaped tablespoonful of the beaten egg white into the cake mixture to slacken the consistency, then gently fold in the remaining beaten egg white until the mixture is just combined. Do not overmix.

7 Spoon into the prepared cups until half full and bake for 15 minutes, until golden. Leave to cool, slightly then turn out on to a rack.

8 To make the icing, mix the ingredients together, adding enough of the water to form a soft liquid icing, and spread it on the cakes until it almost reaches the edges. While the icing is fresh quickly add the decorations, then leave to set.

COOK'S TIP
Remember to match the paper cake cases to the occasion for a special anniversary: silver for a silver wedding, red for a ruby wedding and so on.

Energy 346kcal/1471kJ; Protein 3.3g; Carbohydrate 82.5g, of which sugars 77.4g; Fat 2.6g, of which saturates 0.5g; Cholesterol 57mg; Calcium 53mg; Fibre 0.3g; Sodium 26mg.

Teapot decoration

This pretty teapot cupcake is sure to be a showstopper at any party, whether it's for a child's birthday or for a young-at-heart adult. The decoration is quite time-consuming to make but well worth the effort. Use a basic recipe for the cupcakes.

basic cupcakes (see p14–15)
scraps of sugarpaste
food pastes in pastel colours
small quantity glacé icing
icing (confectioners') sugar,
  for dusting

1 Tint small quantities of sugarpaste lilac, lemon, pink and brown for each component of the teapot and teacup design. Wrap each ball separately and tightly in clear film (plastic wrap) so that it does not dry out. Keep in a cool place.

2 Coat the top of each cake with white glacé icing to fill the case.

3 On sifted icing sugar, roll out a thin circle of white sugarpaste to fit just inside the paper case. Stamp out a circle using a scallop-edge cutter and stick in place while the glacé icing is wet.

4 Roll out a thin layer of lilac sugarpaste for the mat below the teapot. Cut a small circle using a scallop edge cutter.

5 Impress a design in it using a modelling tool and stick in place.

6 To make the body of the teapot, roll a ball of pale yellow paste so that it is smooth all over. Make another smaller ball for the lid. Flatten the bottom edge slightly and stick in place with water. Make a small sausage for the handle and another for the spout. Fix in place with water. Carefully smooth any joins with your fingers.

7 Cut out a flat disc for the saucer. Model a bowl for the cup and fill with glacé icing to represent a drink. Make a sausage handle. The teaspoon is a small sausage rolled thinly at one end and shaped with a ball tool. The cake on the saucer is made of layered sugarpaste balls.

Strawberry cakes

This pretty decorative design has to be assembled just before serving so that the fresh fruit doesn't discolour the sugarpaste topping. All the components can be made ahead of time though for speedy serving. Use a basic cupcake recipe.

basic cupcakes (see p14–15)
strawberry jam
small quantity sugarpaste
pink and green food colouring
2 sizes of strawberry flowers
icing (confectioners') sugar, for
    dusting
fresh strawberries

1 Coat the top of each cupcake with a generous layer of strawberry jam.

2 Tint some sugarpaste pink and roll it out thinly on a surface dusted lightly with icing sugar. Stamp out a circle to fit the top of the cupcake using a round scallop-edge cutter. Stick in place on top of the jam.

3 Tint another small amount of sugarpaste pale leaf green. Roll out and cut out leaves and calyx shapes.

4 Using glacé icing, stick the components in place. Stick a leaf in place on one side of the cupcake top. Decide where the strawberry will go and position the two strawberry flowers close by.

5 Wrap the sugarpaste calyx around the top of the strawberry. Use a blob of jam to hold it in place and stick in position on top of the cupcake just before serving.

Almond cupcakes with grapes

Bunches of marzipan grapes decorate these spectacular tea party cakes, but if you would prefer a simpler decoration you could finish the cakes elegantly with just a single green vine leaf laid on top. Brandy can be substituted for grappa in the recipe.

5 For the marzipan topping, roll out 175g/6oz of marzipan fairly thinly on a board dusted with icing (confectioners') sugar. Using a crinkle-edged cutter, cut 10 circles.

6 Colour 115g/4oz marzipan apple green. Roll it out thinly and cut out 10 vine leaves.

MAKES 10

225g/8oz marzipan
75g/3oz/6 tbsp butter, softened
100g/3½oz/scant ½ cup caster (superfine) sugar
3 eggs, lightly beaten
15ml/1 tbsp grappa
100g/3½oz/scant ½ cup ground almonds
150g/5oz/1¼ cups plain (all-purpose) flour
10ml/2 tsp baking powder
10ml/2 tsp Seville orange marmalade, sieved

For the decoration
500g/1¼lb white marzipan
green and purple food colouring
50g/2oz royal icing
a little sieved apricot jam
10 dried or fresh apple stalks

1 Preheat the oven to 180°C/350°F/Gas 4. Line the cups of a bun tin (pan) with paper cases.

2 Beat the marzipan, butter and sugar together to a smooth, even paste, using an electric mixer. With the whisk running, add the eggs in a very thin stream, beating well until the mixture is very smooth.

3 Fold in the grappa, almonds and flour sifted with the baking powder. Finally, stir in the marmalade.

4 Fill the paper cases a little over half full with the mixture and bake for 20–25 minutes until golden and springy to the touch in the centre. Leave to cool completely on a wire rack, then slice off the cake tops level with the tops of the cases.

7 Colour the remaining marzipan purple and roll it into nine smooth balls for each cake.

8 Heat the apricot jam and brush on the centre of each cake. Press the circles of marzipan on top. Brush the centre of each circle with hot apricot jam and stick on the grapes, stacked to resemble a small bunch, then attach a vine leaf with royal icing and push in an apple stalk.

Energy 572kcal/2404kJ; Protein 10.5g; Carbohydrate 76.9g, of which sugars 65g; Fat 25.7g, of which saturates 6.1g; Cholesterol 81mg; Calcium 122mg; Fibre 2.9g; Sodium 94mg.

Fairy cupcakes

This easy recipe uses a basic mixture. The cakes are decorated with a buttercream topping. The delicate pearlized effect is achieved using edible lustre powder, available from sugarcraft suppliers. Add a tiny silver fairy decoration to complete the magical effect.

MAKES 8–9

175g/6oz/¾ cup butter, softened
175g/6oz/¾ cup caster (superfine) sugar
5ml/1 tsp vanilla extract
4 eggs, lightly beaten
175g/6oz/1½ cups self-raising (self-rising) flour
silver dragées, fairy, and edible lustre powder, to decorate

For the buttercream
75g/3oz/6 tbsp butter, softened
175g/6oz/1½ cups icing (confectioners') sugar, double sifted, plus extra for dusting
½ vanilla pod (bean), split

1 Preheat the oven to 180°C/350°F/ Gas 4. Line the cups of a bun tin (pan) with paper cases.

2 Place the butter and sugar in a large bowl, and beat until light and creamy using an electric mixer. Add the vanilla extract and beat in the eggs in small amounts, beating well after each addition.

3 Sift the flour over and fold it gently into the mixture.

4 Spoon the mixture into the cases and bake for 20 minutes until the cakes are golden brown and the centres feel firm when pressed.

5 Leave the cakes in the tin for 5 minutes to cool, then transfer to a wire rack to cool completely.

6 To make the buttercream, beat the butter with the sugar and vanilla seeds until smooth and fluffy.

7 Spoon a thick blob of buttercream on to the top of each cake and smooth it over the surface, but not right up to the edges. Brush the tops of the cakes with edible lustre powder and top with silver dragées.

Energy 457kcal/1914kJ; Protein 4.9g; Carbohydrate 55.7g, of which sugars 40.9g; Fat 25.4g, of which saturates 15.7g; Cholesterol 148mg; Calcium 65mg; Fibre 0.6g; Sodium 242mg.

Christmas spice cupcakes

Mincemeat, brandy and freshly ground spices are the main ingredients in these delicious celebration cupcakes, which are ideal for those who love the rich spicy flavours of Christmas. The iced cupcake toppings will require a small snowflake or other Christmas themed cutter.

MAKES 14

2 eggs
115g/4oz/½ cup golden caster (superfine) sugar
50ml/2fl oz/¼ cup double (heavy) cream
grated rind of 1 clementine
115g/4oz/⅓ cup mincemeat
115g/4oz/1 cup self-raising (self-rising) flour
2.5ml/½ tsp baking powder
5ml/1 tsp mixed (apple pie) spice
10ml/2 tsp brandy
50g/2oz/4 tbsp butter, melted

For the icing
350g/12oz/3 cups icing (confectioners') sugar, sifted
15ml/1 tbsp hot water
red food colouring

To decorate
175g/6oz sugarpaste
red paste food colouring (or use 115g/4oz pre-coloured red sugarpaste)

1 Preheat the oven to 180°C/350°F/ Gas 4. Line the cups of a bun tin (pan) with paper cases.

2 Lightly beat the eggs with the sugar. Beat the cream into the egg mixture for about 1 minute, then add the grated clementine rind. Fold in the mincemeat. Sift in the flour, baking powder and mixed spice and fold in.

3 Finally add the brandy and the melted butter and stir to combine.

4 Half-fill the paper cases with the batter. Place in the centre of the oven and bake for 12–15 minutes until risen and golden. Test by lightly pressing the centre of the cakes with your fingertips; the sponge should spring back. Leave on a wire rack to cool.

5 To make the icing, mix the sugar with just enough hot water to make a soft icing. Tint one-third of it with the red food colour and spoon over four of the cakes. Ice the remaining cakes with the white icing.

6 Set aside one-third of the sugarpaste and colour the rest red. Roll both out and stamp out 10 red and 4 white snowflakes. Stick one on each cake before the icing sets.

Energy 272kcal/1153kJ; Protein 2g; Carbohydrate 56g, of which sugars 49.7g; Fat 6.1g, of which saturates 3.4g; Cholesterol 40mg; Calcium 43mg; Fibre 0.4g; Sodium 52mg.

Chocolate cupcakes with crème fraîche icing

These simple chocolate cakes have a sweet and sharp crème fraîche icing, which can be made using either dark or white chocolate. Cut the Christmas tree decorations out of contrasting chocolate, and bake the cakes in gold cases to sparkle on the festive table.

MAKES 20

150g/5oz dark (bittersweet)
  chocolate
175ml/6fl oz/³⁄₄ cup single (light)
  cream
5ml/1 tsp vanilla extract
225g/8oz/1 cup golden caster
  (superfine) sugar
200g/7oz/scant 1 cup butter
3 eggs
225g/8oz/2 cups plain (all-purpose)
  flour
20g/³⁄₄oz/2 tbsp unsweetened
  cocoa powder
10ml/2 tsp baking powder

For the icing and decoration
200g/7oz dark (bittersweet) or
  white chocolate
50g/2oz/4 tbsp butter
250ml/8fl oz/1 cup crème fraîche
75g/3oz/³⁄₄ cup icing
  (confectioners') sugar, sifted
225/8oz white or dark (bittersweet)
  chocolate, to decorate

1 Preheat the oven to 190°C/375°F/ Gas 5. Line the cups of two bun tins (pans) with paper cases.

2 Melt the chocolate with the cream over a low heat, stirring constantly. Stir in the vanilla and set aside.

3 Beat the sugar and butter together until light and fluffy, then beat in the eggs one at a time. Sift the flour, cocoa powder and baking powder over the butter mixture and fold in, alternating with the chocolate cream, until the batter is combined.

4 Half-fill the prepared cups and lightly smooth the tops level. Bake for 20–25 minutes, until the centres are firm. Cool on a wire rack.

5 To make the icing, melt the chocolate and butter over a pan of simmering water, stirring, until smooth. Leave to cool a little, then stir in the crème fraîche followed by the sugar. Spread the icing over the cupcakes with a metal spatula.

6 Melt the chocolate for the trees over a pan of simmering water and pour on to a tray lined with baking parchment. Chill until just set, then cut out the shapes and chill again until firm. Stick on to the cakes.

Energy 419kcal/1751kJ; Protein 4.2g; Carbohydrate 43.8g, of which sugars 33.6g; Fat 26.5g, of which saturates 16.4g; Cholesterol 79mg; Calcium 57mg; Fibre 0.5g; Sodium 125mg.

Index